P9-CJC-733

WEATHER VANES

Winnifred E. Short Memorial

J. Morehouse

OTHER BOOKS BY CHARLES KLAMKIN:

Barns: Their History, Preservation, and Restoration
If It Doesn't Work Read the Instructions
How To Buy Major Appliances

WEATHER VANES

The History, Design, and Manufacture of an American Folk Art

CHARLES KLAMKIN

HAWTHORN BOOKS, INC.
PUBLISHERS / *New York*

WEATHER VANES: THE HISTORY, DESIGN, AND MANUFACTURE OF AN AMERICAN FOLK ART.
Copyright © 1973 by Charles Klamkin. Copyright under International and Pan-American Copyright Conventions. All rights reserved, including the right to reproduce this book or portions thereof in any form, except for the inclusion of brief quotations in a review. All inquiries should be addressed to Hawthorn Books, Inc., 260 Madison Avenue, New York, New York 10016. This book was manufactured in the United States of America and published simultaneously in Canada by Prentice-Hall of Canada, Limited, 1870 Birchmount Road, Scarborough, Ontario. Library of Congress Catalog Card Number: 73-352.

1 2 3 4 5 6 7 8 9 10

For Joan, Lynn, and Peter

CONTENTS

ACKNOWLEDGMENTS

I am indebted to many people for help I have received in the preparation of this book. Two sources in particular require special thanks. First, the Shelburne Museum of Shelburne, Vermont, its director, Mr. Sterling D. Emerson, and his dedicated staff. I was received courteously by them and given full access to their records and to their incomparable collection of American weather vanes.

A second invaluable source for information was Mr. Kenneth Lynch, president of Kenneth Lynch and Sons, Incorporated, of Wilton, Connecticut, who graciously shared with me his vast knowledge and expertise in the history and construction of weather vanes. Mr. Lynch, his wife, Cicely, and son, Timothy, enthusiastically contributed to many aspects of the research for this book.

I would also like to thank the following people, who have assisted me in many ways: Mrs. Donald A. Eschenbecker, of Schenectady, New York; Mrs. Betty Friedman, of Woodbury, Connecticut; Miss Sue Warner-Prouty, of New Haven, Connecticut; Mr. Everett Brunncknow, of East Providence, Rhode Island; Mr. Norman T. Worthington, of Providence, Rhode Island; Mr. Cliff Hirsch, of Woodbury, Connecticut; and Mr. Gardner M. Spungin, of New York, New York.

Mr. John Garret Thew, of Norfolk, Connecticut, gave me an appreciation of the craftsmanship involved in fabricating his handmade hollow-body copper weather vanes. He also gave me the use of rare old weather vane catalogs and was most generous in allowing me to photograph his work as well as the vanes made by his late father, Garrett Thew.

My wife, Marian, took time from her busy writing schedule to help organize a vast number of photographs and to edit the text. I am most grateful, also, to Mrs. Elizabeth Backman, who first suggested weather vanes as a subject for a book.

I am also indebted to a large number of people who may have seen a strange man stop his car in front of their houses and point a camera with a huge lens at their roof and who did not phone for the police.

WEATHER VANES

1

WEATHER VANES:
AN AMERICAN FOLK ART

Wind from the east—bad for man and for beast;
Wind from the south is too hot for them both;
Wind from the north is of very little worth;
Wind from the west is the softest and the best.
The (Old) Farmer's Almanack (1851)

When the wind is in the east
Then the sap will run the least
When the wind is in the west
Then the sap will run the best.
New England

Weather vanes have long been recognized as beautiful and representative examples of American folk art. Those made in the late eighteenth century and throughout the nineteenth century have the vigor, charm, and originality that place them among the best of this country's artistic achievements. For the past fifty years the more aware curators have been adding weather vanes to museum collections of folk art and Americana.

Lately weather vanes have become one of the most popular collectors' items among collectors of Americana. The resurgent interest in weather vanes is being catered to by a growing number of dealer-specialists. If anyone has recently attended an antiques show composed of high-quality antiques he cannot have failed to notice how greatly the number of weather vanes on display has proliferated. By merely flipping through the pages of any one issue of the better antiques journals published in this country, one finds as many as a half-dozen spectacular weather vanes being advertised.

One reason for this current surge in the desire to own old weather vanes is that they are works of art. They possess the qualities of good design and hand-craftsmanship, and they express a feeling for this country's history and folklore. Weather vanes are finding their places as wall decorations in the home, as pieces of sculpture, and as garden ornaments. The reason prices are so high is simply that fine old weather vanes have become increasingly rare.

As demand expands for any commodity in limited supply, its price will rise and great effort will be made to satisfy the market. In the case of weather vanes this has led dealers to comb the countryside, scanning rooftops and barn cupolas for saleable examples. The dearth of supply has led also to the outright theft of weather vanes from the buildings they dominate as well as to the manufacture of clever fakes.

The lengths to which some thieves will go to pluck a fine weather vane from a building have become more and more ingenious. With values soaring, it has even become economically feasible to hire helicopters to lift weather vanes from their mountings on rooftops. First reports of thieves using a helicopter to snatch up weather vanes seemed like the beginning of a modern myth that was being passed on from dealer to dealer and from collector to collector. In addition to the expense and risk of making the pilot an accessory to a felony, it would seem impossible to accomplish the vane-napping undetected. Helicopters are frightfully noisy hovering fifty feet or so above the ground, and anyone on the ground seeing or hearing something so conspicuous would certainly be curious to find out what it was doing at treetop level.

These considerations led to the discounting of the tales of aerial skyjacking of weather vanes by those underestimating the nerve and resourcefulness of art thieves. Research, however, has documented at least one weather-vane theft accomplished in this manner. It occurred several years' ago when a large modern eagle weather vane, costing over one thousand dollars, was stolen from the rooftop of the Ottawa Silica Company in Ottawa, Illinois, by persons in a helicopter. This case was confirmed by the manufacturer of the vane, Kenneth Lynch and Sons, Incorporated, which was called upon to construct a replacement for the stolen eagle.

More vulnerable to theft, of course, are valuable weather vanes atop buildings in remote, secluded areas such as farms or vacation dwellings. With the owners away it doesn't require a great deal of effort to place a ladder against a building, climb the roof, and make off with the weather vane. That this has been accomplished fairly frequently, particularly in New England and New York State, can be attested by the number of ads placed by owners offering rewards and seeking to recover stolen weather vanes. These notices appear repeatedly in periodicals directed to the antiques trade.

Weather vanes, as folk art, fall into several definite categories with each depicting traditional motifs. Those most commonly found are domestic animals such as horses, cows, and the ubiquitous rooster or weathercock. Next in popularity is the style incorporating banners, pennants, and arrows of a type most often seen on churches and other public buildings. This type was also used on many elaborate homes in this country in the late nineteenth century. Other typical styles depict various fish from cod to whales, creatures from mythology, patriotic and ecclesiastic symbols, and trade emblems.

The materials from which weather vanes were made varied almost as much as their subjects. Over the years vanes have been fashioned from such simple materials as wooden boards and plain sheet iron to copper, zinc, tin, and brass. Currently, weather vanes are being produced from such modern materials as cast aluminum, stainless steel, and fiber glass. The majority of the old weather vanes found today were made of copper and were produced in the latter half of the nineteenth century by a few active manufacturers located principally in New England.

Although made in large numbers by relatively slow industrial methods, these factory-made weather vanes represent the traditional subjects and exhibit a high level of craftsmanship and design. However, it is the weather vanes that are unique in respect to subject, artist, or the historic building on which they were located that are the most valuable ones of all. These, if they can be properly authenticated, fall into the class of true art treasures and are actively sought by collectors of Americana and museums of folk art. Vanes belonging in this exclusive category may be taken for granted while still in use on the cupola or spire for which they were originally designed. If the building were to be demolished, however, museums and wealthy collectors would compete avidly to secure them.

A few examples of the historic vanes still in their original places are the grasshopper atop Boston's Faneuil Hall, the rooster on the First Church in Cambridge, Massachusetts, and the banner on the "Old North" Church (Christ Church) in Boston. All of these were made by America's first documented weather-vane maker, Shem Drowne. Aside from their excellence of design and execution, their association with America's history places vanes like these beyond price.

The work of our early tinsmiths, coppersmiths, iron-mongers, and wood-carvers can be represented in a collection of old weather vanes. From the most primitive wooden codfish vane to the elaborate gilded eagles, they all tell us something about the men who made them and the families or organizations that ordered them. We also learn the importance to our forefathers of knowing, every minute of the day, which way the wind was blowing.

2

HISTORY OF
WEATHER VANES

The farmer or anyone working out of doors had to know which way the wind was blowing. In this area, where I come from, an east wind meant rain and always there were weather vanes all over the place. Everybody had one, even a little wooden one, up there. . . . Everybody was always looking out the window at the weather vane. But the men who worked outside, they knew quite a lot about the weather. . . . Kids got to know about weather vanes, too. They planned their own activities based on what they knew about the weather.

Anything that the wind would blow or turn made a weather vane. We were always making these arrows from a piece of an old shingle or any old thing we could get a hold of. I must have made a billion of them when I was a kid. We used to worry a hole through with a hot nail held with a pair of pliers and just run a nail down. It would turn on top of a fence post, or if you got really classy, you got up on the barn.

–Kenneth Lynch
Kenneth Lynch and Sons, Inc.
Wilton, Connecticut

Kenneth Lynch and his ancestors have been making weather vanes for over one hundred years. The quotation above suggests how much people relied upon weather vanes before our more up-to-date methods of weather forecasting were developed.

Weather, of course, is one of the most important of all natural phenomena. It influences the planting, growing, and harvesting of our crops; hence the availability and abundance of our food supply. It controls our comfort and directly affects our safety on land, sea, or in the air. Any means of predicting weather was just as useful in our civilization's early history as it is today.

During the millennia preceding the invention of the barometer, the only instrument that could help man predict the weather was the weather vane. The little we know about the first use of weather vanes comes mostly from archeological research. The earliest vane of which we have a record was the one on the Tower of the Winds built by Andronicus in Athens during the first century, B.C. We know from contemporary descriptions that this vane took the form of Triton, a sea god of Greek mythology, who had the head and upper body of a man and the tail of a fish. A pointed wand in the sea god's hand indicated the direction from which the wind was blowing. This vane was cast in bronze. With the Greek passion for architectural proportion we can believe that the figure must have been from four to eight feet long in order to look proper atop a forty-five-foot-high temple. We can also assume that smaller, more simple vanes may have been in service many centuries before this one was made.

There is also archeological evidence of metal weather vanes having been used on the Vikings' ships from approximately the ninth century. These were shaped roughly like a quarter of a circle and pivoted along one straight edge with the other flat portion at the top. This type of vane made its way from ships to the steeples of Scandinavian churches in the tenth and eleventh centuries, and some can still be seen in Norway and Sweden.

About a thousand years ago a papal edict declared that the symbol of a rooster be installed at the top of every church in Christendom. The rooster was to serve to recall Peter's betrayal of Christ in which Jesus said, "I tell thee, Peter, the cock shall not crow this day, before that thou shalt thrice deny that thou knowest me." (Luke 22:34) The cock on the steeple was an admonition to the faithful to come to services so as not to deny Christ as Peter had done.

It is not known exactly when these roosters on the churches were converted to weathercocks or vanes. Literary allusions in Chaucer suggest that cocks were turning with the wind at least by the thirteenth or fourteenth century in England. Logic would indicate that the roosters became weather vanes very quickly because of the eminence of their position on top of the tallest structure in every town. This made it possible to observe the vane without difficulty and from a great distance on a clear day. Curiously, the Roman Catholic churches are no longer capped by weathercocks, and those ecclesiastical roosters that are found today adorn various Protestant houses of worship.

During the middle ages, as the nobility gained ascendancy, or at least equal importance with the church, weather vanes with heraldic motifs began to appear. The insignia of a nobleman's coat of arms, carried on a banner and supported by a rod to keep it unfurled, provided quick recognition of the noble and his retinue to friend and foe. From the banner it was a simple progression to make the insignia in metal and place it on top of a castle for use as a weather vane. Vanes suggesting banners, pennants, and flags remained one of the most popular motifs throughout England and Europe for many centuries. In eighteenth- and nineteenth-century America they were widely used on churches and public buildings, and in the nineteenth century merchant and industrial princes placed them on newly built mansions to give themselves an air of feudal nobility.

While the medieval nobility were permitted to carry their armorial bearings on a square banner, lesser ranks were allowed pennants with single or double tails. This elongated, trailing pennant was called a banneret, and its form became the prototype for a style of weather vane. The long, graceful lines of the banneret lent themselves admirably to weather-vane design. Most of the vanes designed by Sir Christopher Wren, the seventeenth-century English architect, incorporate the feeling of pennants as did the vanes made during the Gothic, Baroque, and Palladian periods of European architecture. Banneret weather vanes also carried over strongly to the period of the Gothic revival in the United States during the nineteenth century.

The better-made weather vanes, or at least the few remaining examples of vanes dating from the seventeenth century in this country, were made abroad and imported by the early settlers. The oldest vane in America of which we have a record is the weathercock made in Holland in 1656 for the Dutch Reformed Church in Albany, New York. This weathercock is still in use and can be viewed on a peak between the twin spires of the First Church in Albany. Among other old American vanes still in existence is a banner with the date 1673 cut into it. This banner is now in the collection of the Concord, Massachusetts, Free Library. Also there is a wooden codfish vane that was originally studded with copper nails (to appear as scales) that once topped Paul Revere's shop and is now on exhibit at the Paul Revere House in Boston.

The making of less sophisticated weather vanes flourished in early rural America. Dependent upon the knowledge of which way the wind was blowing and living too far from the church or town hall to see those vanes, most farmers made their own or hired a local blacksmith to do it for them. In addition to making the traditional rooster, arrow, or banner weather vanes, these workers began fashioning vanes of subjects that were part of their everyday lives. From this period in the latter half of the eighteenth century we see vanes representing Indians, horses, wild animals, and angels. Along the seacoast vanes expressed their builders' concern with nautical matters in the motifs of sailing ships, fish, and seagulls.

After the Revolutionary War patriotic themes became popular, and this country's newly chosen symbol of the eagle became a weather-vane subject, although this took more time to come about than the use of the eagle in other forms of decorative art. Particularly in the latter half of the nineteenth century, eagles carved from wood, hammered out of copper, or cut from iron appeared on public buildings, flagpoles, and houses. As the country expanded to the west, so did the eagle weather vane.

Weather vanes of the latter half of the nineteenth century, made for the most part by specialist manufacturers, are representations of many factors that led to the rapid growth of this country in that period. They are bound up in the history of the great railroad expansion, the development of new and elaborate fire-fighting equipment, the development of industry, the age of farm specialization, and the country's interest in exotic animals of other lands. The latter half of the nineteenth century may well be considered the golden age of weather vanes.

3

HOW WEATHER VANES
ARE MADE

A working weather vane can be made from the simplest materials. A pointed stick swinging on a nail will indicate wind direction as efficiently as the most elaborate gold-leafed eagle. Although many fine early weather vanes were cut or whittled from wood, relatively few remain in reasonably good condition. Softer woods such as pine were often used because they were easier to carve, but continual exposure to the elements made their preservation precarious.

Metal vanes are obviously more durable, and weather vanes have been made from practically every kind of metal imaginable. The earliest European weather vanes were made of iron, copper, and bronze, since those were the metals workers had most access to. The most simple metal weather vane to construct is made of a flat sheet cut to the desired shape. Copper, since it is relatively soft, can be cut and shaped quite easily. A thin sheet of iron can be cut with a chisel and hammer and, depending upon the skill of the artisan, can be worked into elaborate designs with cut-out spaces within the design.

Early German, Scandinavian, and English weather vanes were made mostly of iron, while the French used a great deal of zinc. In the American colonies the new settlers introduced weather vanes made in the same manner, styles, and materials to which they were accustomed in the Old World. The Germans in Pennsylvania cut weather vanes from iron in the shape of roosters as well as Indians, which, legend claims, were supposed to represent the desire of the colonists to live in peace with their native neighbors.

In order for the iron vanes to be cut out more easily, the flat parts were made from stock that was rolled quite thin. The larger of these flat pieces were riveted to wrought iron braces to stiffen and support them. This was also done with flat copper vanes and was the principal method of constructing the banneret type of weather vane that was made commercially.

In New England copper weather vanes began to make their appearance in the eighteenth century, and the earliest authenticated weather vane is Shem Drowne's large copper Indian, which was made in 1716. Copper weather vanes can be made in several ways. They can be cut from flat stock and mounted as a silhouette, or flat parts of copper can be added to carved wooden vanes for use as tail feathers on a weathercock or fins on a fish. The more elaborate use of copper is involved in the making of hollow-bodied figures either in the half- or full-round. These are both made from two pieces of copper beaten into molds representing both sides of the figure. Then the two halves are joined together to form the completed image. In the full-round body the molds are deep enough to provide the finished object with natural thickness and contours.

In order to make the hollow mold into which the copper is beaten, one first has to make a wooden model of the desired finished object. The success of the completed copper vane depends upon the craftsmanship of the carving. After the wooden model is made, it is sawed into sections suitable for the making of molds for the copper parts. In a simple design such as a rooster the wood model need only be cut in half from top to bottom. The models for ambitious subjects such as eagles, horses and buggies, or ships would have to be cut into several sections in order to make suitable molds.

The wooden portions of the model are then used to make hollow molds of cast iron. Once the iron molds are cast hundreds and hundreds of copper pieces can be made from them before they suffer any deterioration. A thin sheet of copper is laid over the mold and beaten down into it until the copper conforms to the shape of the mold. Efforts to perform this operation with a hydraulic press have been attempted without any real success. Any means other than hand-hammering does not achieve the maximum surface detail.

One method of shaping the rounded copper weather-vane parts is a technique whereby lead is poured into the iron mold resulting in a lead casting of the mold. This casting is then removed from the mold, and a sheet of copper is placed between the mold and the casting like a sandwich. A worker hammers on the lead casting so as not to damage the copper, and this method is said to produce a more faithful rendering of the detail in the mold.

Some contemporary copper vanes are being made in a similar manner. There are shops that use a lead casting to press several sheets of copper at once into old or new molds under hydraulic pressure. Several sets of parts can be made in a single operation in this manner, but obviously only the first sheet of copper in direct contact with the mold will have the proper fidelity.

A more typical way to hammer out weather vanes was to use small cloth bags filled with two or three pounds of lead shot. As a piece of copper was being beaten down into the iron mold, these bags were placed strategically to prevent the copper from shifting laterally or bouncing up and down. The lead-filled bags acted only as a ballast and were never struck with the mallet.

After the necessary parts of the copper molds are formed, they are trimmed, matched, and soldered together. Then the joints are filed and buffed smooth. All that then remains to be done is to mount the weather vane onto a suitable support and spindle. Although the process just described is the way that most three-dimensional copper weather vanes have been made in commercial factories, it is not accurate to call them mass-produced objects. Machinery does not lend itself to their manufacture, and even though they have been and are being made in large quantities, half-round and full-round weather vanes of copper can fairly be thought of as handcrafted artifacts.

Hollow-bodied copper weather vanes can also be made by another method that does not require the use of molds. This is the repoussé process in which a sheet of copper is worked into shape with the use of tools directly from an artist's design. As can be imagined, this requires considerable skill on the part of the worker, who must visualize the finished part in the blank metal and be able to shape it and provide it with detail with only a hammer and assorted metal-working tools. The various parts must still be made separately and, when joined, match perfectly. This is the way any monumentally sized copper weather vane must be made and was the process used by Shem Drowne to make his outsize vanes. The same process is used to make the larger weather vanes that are produced today. The repoussé technique in weather-vane making is borrowed from the goldsmiths and silversmiths who have been familiar with it for centuries.

In the introduction to J. W. Fiske's weather-vane catalog of 1893 particular emphasis is placed on the fact that the Fiske vanes were made only of copper, brass tubing, and wrought iron.

> My Vanes are all MADE OF COPPER and not a combination of zinc and copper like other vanes on the market. . . . GILDED WITH THE FINEST GOLD LEAF; [Fiske weather vanes] will not corrode, and will keep bright for a long time.

I would caution my customers and the public against being deceived by Vanes which are now being made, copied after my designs, some of which are made of SHEET ZINC, AND COVERED WITH A THIN SOLUTION OF COPPER WITH ZINC TUBING. Unlike my Vanes which are made of Sheet Copper, and mounted with brass tubing.

We can gather from Fiske's warning that late in the nineteenth century successful weather-vane designs were being pirated and low-priced copies were being made. Zinc is softer than copper and, while less durable, is easier to work. Vanes made with zinc would also cost less to fabricate. Once a vane was covered with gold leaf, it would be difficult for a buyer to know what the underlying metal was. For the collector of late nineteenth-century weather vanes Mr. Fiske's warning is still valid. At that time, as now, the better weather vanes were made of sheet copper.

Gold leaf will enhance the appearance of a weather vane and help slow down the action of the weather and the corrosive elements of the atmosphere on its surface. In time, however, the gold leaf will disappear and the unprotected weather vane will be left to acquire a natural patina. A copper weather vane that has been exposed long enough to achieve a mellow greenish-gray patina is generally more pleasing to the eye than the bright gold finish it had when it left the shop.

Modern weather-vane makers are not as enthusiastic about the combination of copper and wrought iron in the construction of the vanes they are making today. It is felt that the two metals set up an electrolytic reaction that tends to accelerate the corrosion of copper, especially on the sheathing of the roof. Also, wrought iron will eventually rust and interfere with the freedom of movement needed to permit the vane to swing freely in the wind. Therefore, stainless steel is the material of choice for spindles and bearings when the long, trouble-free operation of a weather vane is a prime concern.

Aside from copper and wrought iron, many contemporary weather vanes are being made of aluminum and other materials that were unavailable not too many years ago. Aluminum is fairly durable, especially when protected with a good quality enamel, and lends itself to extreme ease of forming. It can be poured into molds or stamped from dies and, except for large subjects in the full-round, is suitable for moderate-sized solid body vanes.

Fiber glass is another innovation in the making of weather vanes. The vanes that top the Howard Johnson restaurants and motor lodges as well as the familiar figure of Colonel Sanders on the Kentucky Fried Chicken outlets are molded from this relatively new material. Both aluminum and fiber glass lend themselves to the mass production of weather vanes stamped or pressed out in cookie-cutter fashion. As such it is doubtful whether they will ever move into the collectible category except as artifacts of American business history.

Mechanically, of course, a weather vane is a very simple device. All that would appear necessary to make one work properly is a pivoted construction that presents a greater surface to the wind on one end than the other. There is, however, the additional consideration of balance. Normally, there is a great deal more weight in back of the spindle of a weather vane than there is in the front. That is the part that is built up to catch the wind. In order to swing freely, the front and back of the vane must be balanced equally from the point at which the vane pivots. This is not difficult to do with an arrow or other flat subjects, but with a hollow-body horse, rooster, eagle, or other more complicated shape, balancing requires a certain degree of expertise.

Lead is the metal most frequently used inside the front end of hollow weather vanes to achieve balance. The molten lead must be carefully measured and poured into the hollow vane as far forward as possible. To do this, either a small section is left open to be soldered into place later, or a hole is made in the vane and covered and repaired after the ballast is introduced. If this is carefully done, the final gold-leafing will cover all traces of the hole. As the lead is introduced, it is desirable that it be cooled rapidly. This is done by holding a wet cloth against the outer surface, but some older workers feel that a potato cut in half and pressed against the copper works better. Some hollow-body copper horse and cow weather vanes are fitted with cast iron heads to achieve balance.

All the care and time invested in balancing a weather vane will be wasted if the vane is not fitted properly to its spindle. Early weather-vane makers overcame the rust hazard of wrought iron by learning to fit the spindles to the sockets loosely. If the parts are not fitted too tightly, any rust formed will be ground away by the constant movement of the vane. The ends of the wrought iron spindles were also pointed in order to present less surface for friction between spindle and socket.

Some later vanes are equipped with bronze bearings, and a number of thoughtful manufacturers today furnish a stainless steel ball to insert between the spindle shaft and the socket on the weather vane. Ball bearings mounted in a regular circular race have been tried, and although they promote freedom of movement, they can present difficulties. Unless unusually well protected, bird droppings or moisture causing rust will cause them to freeze up.

This potential trouble was apparently overcome in one weather vane as evidenced in this excerpt from a letter to the Citizens Bank of Providence, Rhode Island. This letter was from the C. G. Brunncknow Company of Providence and concerns the ship weather vane built by them over fifty years ago for the bank's office on Westminster Street:

It [the ship weather vane] is constructed entirely of copper, brass and bronze except for the lead ballast and it is mounted on a $1^{15}/_{16}$″ steel shaft weighing 160 pounds. It turns on an automobile ball bearing. The hull is copper and weighs 46 pounds. Eleven pounds of lead were used for ballast to balance it. The mast and cross arms are of brass tubing. A total of 186 feet of $\frac{1}{8}$″, $\frac{3}{16}$″, $\frac{1}{4}$″ and $\frac{3}{8}$″ bronze rope was used in the rigging. It is 6′2″ long and 4′6″ high from keel to top of mast. Two hundred and thirty-nine man hours of skilled labor were required to build and mount it. It was mounted in place on April 26, 1921 and, to our knowledge, has never required any attention or service and survived the hurricane of 1938 with no damage and with no loss of its efficient operation.

The fine craftsmanship required to make good weather vanes has not diminished in the two-and-one-half centuries since Shem Drowne made his vanes in Boston. Essentially the same basic principles of proportion, balance, and artistic integrity apply as do the respect for sound materials and honest workmanship.

Photograph of Citizens Bank,
Providence, Rhode Island, ship
weather vane. Photo taken in 1921
before vane was installed. Man at
left is Charles Hallberg, shop foreman.
At right is Jacob Leibo, workman who
executed model. (*C. G. Brunncknow
Company*)

Photo taken in 1890 shows two banneret
vanes already mounted on cupolas
being displayed on float celebrating
one hundredth anniversary of
Pawtucket, Rhode Island, cotton
industry. Large man in center of float is
C. G. Brunncknow. (*C. G. Brunncknow
Company*)

14

Copper, brass, and bronze ship vane made in 1921 by the C. G. Brunncknow Company for the Citizens Bank in Providence, Rhode Island. Vane is six feet two inches long, four feet six inches tall, and required 239 skilled man hours to construct.

Wrought iron weathercock made in 1670. (*Henry Francis Du Pont Winterthur Museum*)

Pennsylvania German banneret. Wrought iron with star and heart cutout and date, 1808. (*Shelburne Museum*)

16

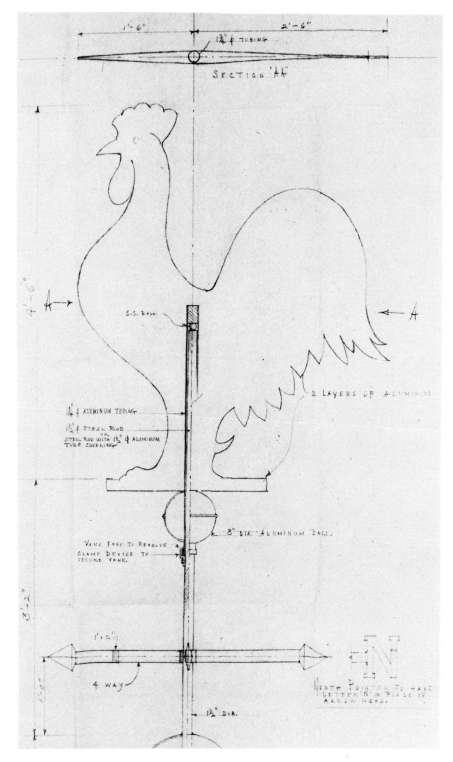

Drawing of four-foot six-inch aluminum
weathercock made by Kenneth Lynch
and Sons, Incorporated, for Pittsburgh
Theological Seminary in Pittsburgh,
Pennsylvania.

Lynch Company shop drawing of replica of vane on Philadelphia's Independence Hall. Executed for Russellville branch of the Benjamin Franklin Savings and Loan Association of Portland, Oregon.

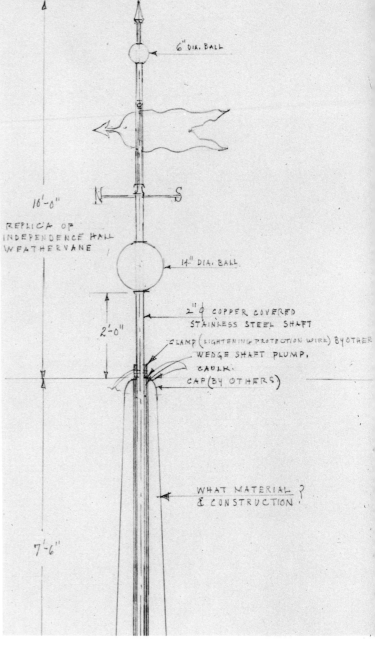

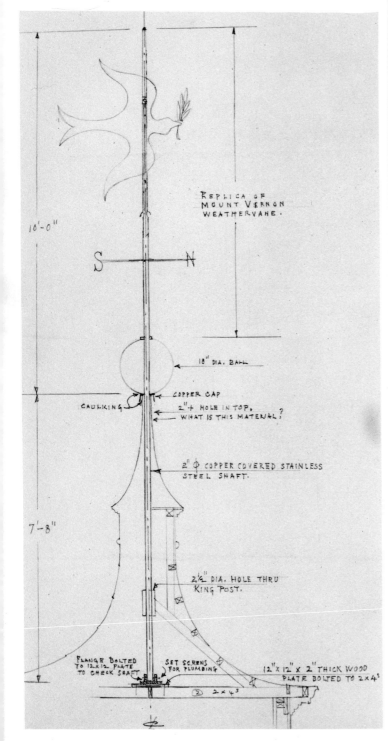

Architectural plan for installation of replica of vane in Mount Vernon for branch of Benjamin Franklin Savings and Loan Association at Lake Oswego, Oregon. Made by Kenneth Lynch and Sons, Incorporated.

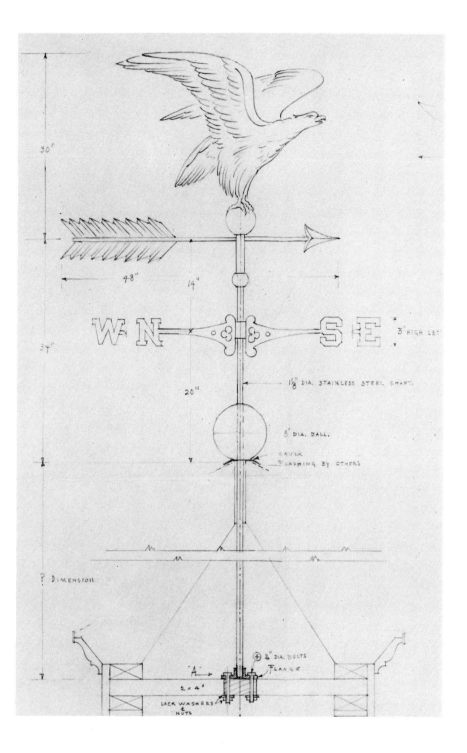

Scale drawing of four-foot eagle vane
built by Kenneth Lynch and Sons,
Incorporated, for the Pickneyville Bank,
Pickneyville, Illinois.

Kenneth Lynch showing one half of iron mold used to fashion full-bodied copper grasshopper vane.

Mr. Lynch hammering copper sheet into iron grasshopper mold. Hammer strikes wooden peg, which is softer than the copper and will not injure it. Cloth bags at the right are weighted with lead shot to keep copper from shifting in the mold or bouncing up and down.

Partially completed copper grasshopper is removed from mold to check detailing.

4

WEATHER-VANE MAKERS

Many of the earliest weather-vane makers were amateur carvers and town blacksmiths and will remain anonymous forever. Although examples of their work have lasted and can be found in many museums and on a few rooftops throughout the country, few weather vanes from the seventeenth or eighteenth century were documented or marked by their makers in any way. The early weather vanes were produced and erected because they were a necessary object for the sailor and the farmer and were not thought to be especially important works of art unless they were being made for an important building. It is these landmark weather vanes for which records of the makers often still exist.

Four weather vanes still exist that were made by America's first master vane-maker, Shem Drowne, of Boston. Born in 1683, Drowne was a metal-worker and wood-carver who executed copper vanes that were unique at the time for their large size and innovative design. Three of Shem Drowne's vanes are still in use. One is a five-foot-high, hollow-bodied rooster weighing over 170 pounds. Made in 1722 for the New Brick Church in Boston, it has found its way to the steeple of The First Church in Cambridge, Massachusetts.

Another famous church weather vane is Drowne's banner-shaped vane on Boston's Old North Church installed in 1740. This is the church in which the lanterns that prompted Paul Revere's famous ride were hung. By virtue of its significance as an historic landmark and as a perch for a Shem Drowne weather vane, it was a calamity of national proportions when the steeple of Old North Church was blown down by a hurricane in August 1954. Money was raised by public subscription, and the Kenneth Lynch firm donated its services to rebuilding the famous weather vane.

Mr. Lynch found that most of the copper in the vane, which was hammered out over two hundred years ago, could still be salvaged. However, time and the steeple's fall had seriously damaged the associated ironwork, such as the heavy spindle and the delicate scroll work. New parts were fashioned from the original designs, and the completely restored steeple and weather vane were replaced on the church the next year.

Mr. Lynch relates:

> As a sidelight on this job there was a copper shroud on the top of that steeple; evidently the metal had been made in Paul Revere's shop. It was stamped P. REVERE. I realized how important this piece of metal was and it was agreed that I could have a piece of the copper. I did all this work for them free. We took the Revere signature off and the Lantern Society which controls the church has it on exhibition in the museum there. . . . On a Friday afternoon, with the Governor of Massachusetts there, I took this fragment and in a clean crucible we alloyed it with five hundred pounds of gilding metal. I was given two hundred and fifty pounds and the Revere Copper and Brass Company received the same amount. They were going to make commemorative medals or coins out of theirs. I had mine made into bead necklaces by the Bead Chain Company.

Although a complete restoration was done on the North Church vane after the 1954 hurricane, a photograph of the steeple taken in January 1972 shows the double pennant tail of the vane to have been severely twisted and the finial rod over the vane, which supports a crown, to have been bent out of plumb. When this photograph was recently brought to Mr. Lynch's attention, he immediately contacted the rector of the church and offered to repair the vane at no charge if it could be brought to his shop. Since the building is an historic landmark, the United States Coast Guard may supply a helicopter to remove the vane, see that it is shipped to the Lynch factory, and replace it when the work is done.

The Shem Drowne weather vane, no longer in place, is a large copper image of an Indian and was made in 1716. In a story by Nathaniel Hawthorne entitled *Drowne's Wooden Image*, the vane is described as follows:

> One of his productions, an Indian chief, gilded all over, stood during the better part of a century on the cupola of Province House, bedazzling the eyes of those who looked upward, like an angel in the sun.

The Province House was, for a time, the residence of the governors sent by England to rule the Massachusetts Bay Colony. It was torn down in 1922 and the vane removed to the Massachusetts Historical Society, where it can still be seen.

Drowne's most famous weather vane is the grasshopper still atop Boston's Faneuil Hall. The vane was made in 1749 of copper and has eyes of green glass. It was a copy of the weather vane on London's Royal Exchange. At least one other copy of this vane was made by Drowne for a home belonging to Peter Faneuil, and weather-vane manufacturers are still today producing their copies of the famous grasshopper.

Weather vanes made by James Lombard, a nineteenth-century Maine wood-carver, have been recognized as highly desirable examples of native folk art. The most distinguishing features of Lombard weather vanes are the stylized versions of hens and roosters, particularly the imaginative treatment of the tail feathers. Simple in design and execution, Lombard's weather vanes were sawed from pine planks with wooden legs attached separately. Many of these vanes were finished in a yellow paint used to simulate the gold leaf applied to the metal vanes of the time. Born in 1865, Lombard operated a farm in Bridgeton, Maine, most of his adult life. Most of his weather vanes are attributed to his earlier years, and their distribution over a sizable area of Maine indicates that he may have been an itinerant weather-vane maker in his youth.

Prior to 1850 weather vanes were produced by individual craftsmen or amateurs and made from the material closest at hand. A farmer, his son, or a hired man would carve or saw a vane from a piece of scrap board, or the local blacksmith would cut out a silhouette vane from a piece of sheet iron. These simply made, individualistic vanes have great appeal today and are avidly sought by collectors.

Beginning in the middle of the nineteenth century the making of weather vanes passed to a great extent from the individual craftsman to the factories set up for their large-scale manufacture. The most active companies in that period were clustered around either Boston or New York City. The Massachusetts companies were Cushing and White and its more widely known successor, L. W. Cushing & Sons; J. Harris & Son; W. A. Snow; and John A. Whim. Working in New York were the J. W. Fiske Company, J. L. Mott, and E. G. Washburne & Company. J. W. Fiske is still being operated in Paterson, New Jersey, by descendants of its founder.

One of the earliest manufacturers of weather vanes in Massachusetts was A. L. Jewell and Company. This company was begun in 1852 and continued until 1865 when Mr. Jewell and his partner fell off a scaffold and were killed. The business was then taken over by the firm of Cushing and White and continued under this name until 1872 when it became the L. W. Cushing & Sons Company.

Cushing did not solicit business outside of the New England area but sold a few vanes in New York State. Cushing continued in business until 1933 when it, like many other old American firms, succumbed to the Great Depression.

Many of the gilded copper full-round vanes that are found today in museum collections are illustrated in the Cushing and White circular that would date, of course, between 1865 and 1872. This circular shows that the variety of motifs used by all of the great weather-vane makers in the latter half of the nineteenth century were made by Cushing and White, including the less often seen butterfly and peacock vanes.

The firm of E. G. Washburne & Company is still operating in Danvers, Massachusetts, after having passed through the hands of a long-time employee of the original company, a Mr. Charles Kessler. Kessler was a wiry little man who, by virtue of longevity and loyalty, acquired the Washburne name and assets in lieu of back wages after there were no longer any Washburnes left to carry on the business.

Mr. Kessler was interviewed by *The New Yorker* magazine in 1964, when he was eighty-one years old. In that interview he stated,

> In 1853, Isaiah Washburne started E. G. Washburne & Company in a second floor shop at 708 Broadway. He was a friend of Duncan Phyfe, and his son, E. G., who inherited the business, was a friend of J. P. Morgan.
>
> We did all the vanes for the big estates that were going up then, and when I say "big estate" I mean that besides the main house there would be a superintendent's house, a gardener's cottage, a laundry, a garage, and, of course, a stable and carriage house—and they'd all have vanes on the roof. Today what happens? The estates get broken up into subdivisions, and the subdivision houses are all topped off with TV antennas. To make matters worse, when people do buy vanes, they buy the kind that are stamped out by machine, slap, slap, a hundred and fifty a day.

For about forty years up to 1956, when the Washburne tools and dies were sold and moved to Massachusetts, Kessler and his wife made all the Washburne weather vanes. In two rooms over a store on Fulton Street in New York City, Kessler hammered out the copper vanes in the old Washburne molds while his wife did the gold-leafing.

The weather vanes made by these firms during the late nineteenth and early twentieth centuries covered a vast number of eagles, horses, roosters, cows, bannerets, and arrows. All of the factory-made vanes from this period are highly collectible now that the supply of handmade weather vanes has all but disappeared.

Within the past fifty years important weather vanes have been made by companies whose skill in metal-working was not confined to weather vanes only. Among these are the vanes made by the Samuel Yellin Company of Philadelphia. Samuel Yellin was a Polish immigrant who became this country's most talented iron-worker. Until his death in 1940 Mr. Yellin's work was in demand by architects for the finest houses, museums, churches, and universities. When called upon to supply grilles, gates, and other ornamental pieces for a project, Yellin would also be asked to supply wrought iron weather vanes as part of the contract. Some of his weather vanes can be seen at Yale and Princeton universities and on many buildings, of course, in and around Philadelphia. The Yellin tradition of fine ironwork is currently being carried on by his son, Harvey, who is still executing important ironwork commissions.

Kenneth Lynch and Sons, Incorporated, of Wilton, Connecticut, is, of course, headed by the previously quoted Mr. Kenneth Lynch, who joined the family business in 1917. The Lynch family had been blacksmiths and metal-workers in the United States since the middle of the nineteenth century with weather-vane making always occupying a large portion of their output. Mr. Lynch, who has been president of the company since 1928, is a master ironworker, armorer, and weather-vane maker. Over the past forty-six years Mr. Lynch has made every kind and style of weather vane imaginable. Besides supplying the traditional hollow-body copper vanes of eagles, roosters, horses, cows, and other animals, he developed many original weather-vane subjects. Some of these he designed himself, and others were done by Andrew Crowell, who has worked for the Lynch firm for over forty years. From time to time Mr. Lynch has hired talented artists to furnish designs for unusual weather vanes.

One artist employed by Lynch for a special commission was the French sculptor Pierre Bourdel, whose father was also a sculptor and a student of Rodin. Bourdel designed a weather vane for the Newport, Rhode Island, mansion of Vernor Z. Reid, a copper tycoon. This vane was a huge affair executed in the 1930s out of copper and stainless steel, and it represented the sea god Neptune in his shell chariot being pulled by three sea horses. The shell was more than three feet high, and the sea horses were five feet long. The figure of Neptune was approximately the same height. Unfortunately, this formidable weather vane was lost along with a good deal of the house in the 1938 hurricane that inflicted heavy damage on most of New England.

In association with architects this is the type of large-scale, specially designed work in which the Lynch firm is presently engaged. Although offering a very complete catalog of hundreds of weather-vane styles, their principal enthusiasm is for the unusual or monumental weather vane that few other workers are willing or capable of undertaking. As an example the Lynch firm built a tremendous gilded copper eagle weather vane that is twelve feet long from beak to tail for the Lawrence, Massachusetts, Town Hall. Building such a large, hollow structure calls for considerable engineering skill in the vane's reinforcement. This problem was solved by using hollow tubing as armatures to support the hammered copper body and wingspread.

There are a number of other shops and individual craftsmen turning out weather vanes of original design using traditional methods. One such is John Garrett Thew of Norfolk, Connecticut. Mr. Thew makes hand-hammered copper vanes in limited, signed, and numbered series. Working from forms that he carves from wood, he makes a hollow iron mold into which copper sheets are beaten to take the shape of the mold. Further handwork is required to bring up on the surface of the copper the detailing each subject calls for.

Through sales agents Mr. Thew's work is sold in fine stores across the country, and while not inexpensive now, the Thew vanes will obviously come into the category of collectible weather vanes in a few years. They are marked examples of weather vanes made in the true tradition of American folk art, where the maker's time is of less importance than the quality of the product. Mr. Thew's father, Garrett Thew, was also a vane-maker who worked in the silhouette style of the 1920s and 1930s.

Making amusing weather vanes is the hobby of Cliff Hirsch, a building contractor in Woodbury, Connecticut. He makes large weather vanes of scrap material, mostly with humorous themes. He has made one for an obstetrician of a doctor chasing a stork and another of a settler about to be scalped by an Indian. Mr. Hirsch's weather vanes are painted in lifelike detail, and because they are quite large, some six or seven feet long, they are built to swing on old automobile axle bearings that Mr. Hirsch picks up in the junkyards. Vanes made by people like Mr. Hirsch recall the most desirable aspects of the American primitives, and it will not be too long before they become a part of our folk art.

Most of the small, black, painted weather vanes we see on new houses today were bought from a lumber yard or building supply dealer and are made of cast aluminum. One of the largest makers of this kind of vane is the Whitehall Metal Studio Incorporated, in Montague, Michigan. While the vanes they supply work perfectly well, there is little to distinguish them artistically. However, because they are relatively inexpensive, they do allow those people to own weather vanes who could not otherwise afford them.

Neptune driving three sea horses. Bronze, copper, stainless steel. Designed by Pierre Bourdel for Newport, Rhode Island, mansion and built by Kenneth Lynch and Sons, Incorporated. Destroyed in New England hurricane in 1938. Eight feet in length.

The makers of the early primitive vanes such as this iron weathercock are usually unknown today.

Banneret vane on Boston's Old North
Church made by Shem Drowne in
mid-eighteenth century. Vane was
completely restored in 1954 after steeple
fell in hurricane. Present condition
of bent pennant and finial unexplained
but will be repaired after vane is
removed by use of helicopter.

Most famous American weather vane
ever made. Copper grasshopper with
green glass eyes made by Shem Drowne
in 1749 for Faneuil Hall in Boston.

Cushing and White illustrated circular
printed sometime between 1865 and
1872 shows variety of designs made by
that company. (*Shelburne Museum*)

Vane made in 1892 by Fiske Company
illustrates "the pen is mightier than the
sword." This vane was probably used
for schools and libraries.

COPPER WEATHER VANES
Gilded with Gold Leaf

Manufacturers "borrowed" motifs and
designs from one another. This quill vane
is a 1920s Washburne design. It
was made in six sizes from one and a
half to six feet long.

Pen

No. 159	1½ feet long	$10.00
No. 160	2 feet long	13.00
No. 161	3 feet long	22.00
No. 162	4 feet long	32.00
No. 163	5 feet long	50.00
No. 164	6 feet long	70.00

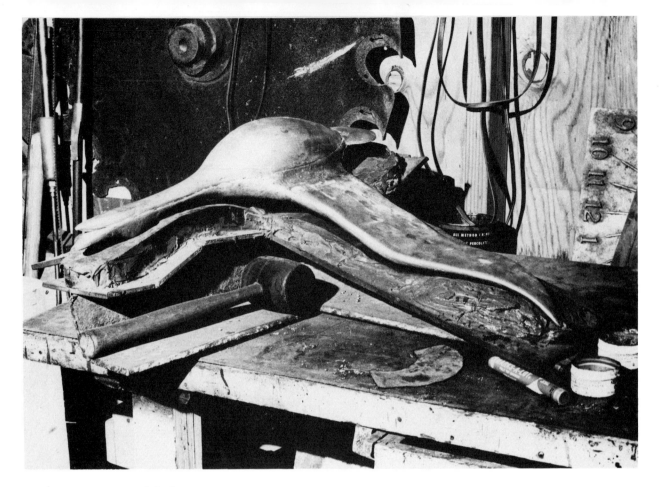

Reassembled wood model of goose vane
resting in one half of mold used to
form copper body of vane.

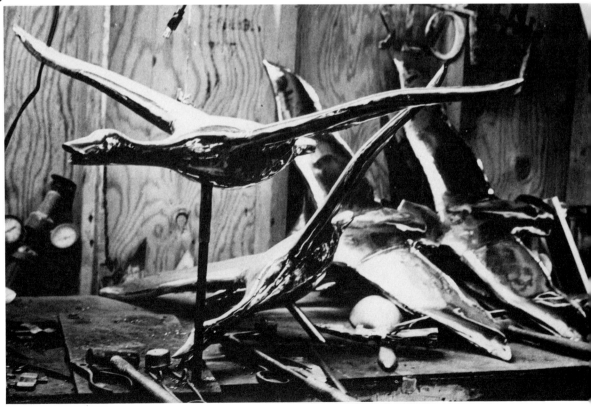

Four goose vanes, a normal week's
production, lie on bench in John Garrett
Thew's workshop.

32

John Garrett Thew, of Norfolk, Connecticut, holding hollow-body copper goose weather vane. He makes these in a limited, signed, and numbered series.

Photograph of mark on the goose vanes made by Mr. Thew. Characters are punched into copper surface on underside of wing.

JOHN GARRET THEW
NORFOLK, CONN.

OCT. 1972   NO. 99

Weather-vane arrows and spindles are stacked against window in the workshop of John Garrett Thew.

Mr. Thew's goose vane mounted on his house complete with arrow and cardinal points. Vane has already begun to acquire patina, and photograph shows where pieces were soldered together for assembly.

34

Vane made of scrap and "found" materials by Cliff Hirsch of Woodbury, Connecticut. Vane rotates on auto axle bearings.

Vane made by Cliff Hirsch is large scale and of heavy construction. Brightly painted.

5

SILHOUETTE VANES

There are "sleepers" in almost every category of collecting, and weather vanes are no exception. Following World War I there was a great amount of building in the United States of moderately priced single-family dwellings. Construction was interrupted to a large extent by the Depression of 1929 but resumed after the country had recovered and continued until the world was once again at war.

While the builders of the great mansions added elaborate and expensive weather vanes to turrets and rooftops, the smaller houses required some sort of roof ornament in order to acquire a "finished" appearance. Weather-vane manufacturers provided a style of vane that was smaller in scale than the full-bodied copper vanes previously made, and these required less handwork. Obviously, these vanes, which were made for single-family middle-class dwellings, also had to be less expensive than the elaborate vanes. The manufacturers went back to the two-dimensional silhouette vanes of the early folk artist and made many fanciful and amusing weather vanes that could be produced in some quantity and required less handwork in their manufacture.

The art of silhouette-making goes back to ancient times. Silhouette portraits were an extremely popular method of recording likenesses of persons at the end of the eighteenth century, and the technique was used and embellished upon throughout the nineteenth century. Paper and a sharp knife or scissors were all the materials needed for the talented artist to produce the facial characteristics of the model, but the art faded into oblivion after 1820, when a silhouette machine that could produce likenesses mechanically was invented. Silhouettes were still popular, but they did not require great talent on the part of the artist.

At the beginning of this century there were few trained artists who could see their subjects in simple black outline, and photography had made the necessity for portrait silhouettes obsolete. For a while the weather-vane manufacturers revived an art that was all but dead and adapted the technique to metal.

Silhouette art was revived by the weather-vane makers of the early twentieth century as a means of providing subjects that were contemporary and that would have a wide appeal so that they would sell in quantity. The artists who designed these metal vanes were faced with special problems that the scissors and paper silhouette artists did not have. The vanes, cut from sheet brass, iron, and copper, would be seen only from a distance, and the outlines and interior cuts had to be simple. Detail had to be kept to a minimum, but it was important that the vane represent its subject matter perfectly. In addition, the vanes had to have perfect balance so that they would swing freely once they were mounted on the shaft. In the two-dimensional metal cut-outs there would be no opportunity for the manufacturer to weight one end of the vane as was frequently done in the manufacture of full-bodied vanes.

The silhouette weather vanes that especially appealed to the small home builder of the twenties were those that told a story. A great variety of genre scenes was designed, and the simple weathercock, fish, horse, or cow were no longer popular. Instead, scenes of America, some of them with regional appeal, were used as weather-vane subjects. A covered wagon being pulled by weary oxen was a popular vane in the Midwest and the West. A stage coach, pulled by four prancing horses, was also a popular subject. The farmer could still order a weather vane with a horse motif, but in the twenties he could have a cutout figure of a mare with her foal. The sailing-ship vanes of the old days were also made in the new silhouette vanes, but for the modern home builder who lived near the water a contemporary sailboat was more popular than a schooner.

These twentieth-century weather vanes were relatively inexpensive, and humorous subjects were sometimes used. A vane of the Three Bears, each holding his bowl of porridge, was made by the Kenneth Lynch Company. The same company also made a vane of "Old Dobbin" pulling his weary passenger. E. G. Washburne & Company made a vane that has an outline of a witch on a broomstick and a rather strange quarter-moon profile. Washburne also produced a genre scene of a farmer hoeing his crops with chickens pecking at the plants in back of him while an obviously ineffectual scarecrow balances the opposite end of the vane. Another Washburne vane is a design of a bull chasing a frightened milk-maid. Many of these early twentieth-century weather vanes, no longer so essential in announcing wind direction, provided a smile to passersby.

Farm scenes were made in some quantity although these were now mostly multifigured silhouettes that "told a story." Lynch's "Harried Farmer" shows a caricature of the farmer being pursued by a fierce bull. The usual tranquil cow stood in silhouette under a tree in a vane called "Green Pastures," and a vane made to appeal to homeowners in the West showed a farmer at his plow, which was being pulled by two strong horses. "Pony Express" was another silhouette obviously made to appeal to westerners. The pony and his rider are shown running through desert rock and cactus.

The use of metal as a material for silhouette weather vanes required less skill on the part of the craftsmen, but a very special talent was needed by the artist who designed them. Surprisingly detailed designs were used, and it is obvious that some artists had a better grasp of the medium than others. Most of the designs were executed on paper by talented freelance artists, and there seems to have been less copying from one manufacturer to another with the more complicated silhouette weather vane patterns, although some of the simpler designs were adapted by all.

One of the most colorful of these freelance silhouette artists who worked in the first quarter of this century was a dapper Englishman whose name was Teddy Tiffin. Mr. Tiffin, who died in 1935, had been Lily Langtry's personal secretary and had accompanied the famous singer for years as she made her international tours. After Miss Langtry's death, Tiffin ended up in the United States, quite poor, with only his ability to sketch and draw to keep him in whiskey and cigarettes. Settling in New York City, Tiffin sold many of his sketches to Kenneth Lynch, who considers him to have been one of the finest pen and ink artists he has ever known. Mr. Lynch helped to support Teddy Tiffin in his declining years by buying his sketches, which were then adapted to silhouette weather vanes.

The Tiffin drawings were meticulously detailed, full-scale renderings of subjects popular with society people in the late 1920s. Most had to do with the leisure activities of the wealthy such as hunting, golf, and polo. However, the Tiffin designs were all executed in silhouette style vanes that were inexpensive enough to be purchased for use on smaller houses and barns. Tiffin was a master at foreshortening, a difficult accomplishment in the art of silhouette, and would work for hours to get the proper curve in a boot or the exact detail of its laces. Where it is required in the design, Tiffin's patterns have great movement and strength and a three-dimensional quality. Tiffin also sold drawings to the Todhunter Company in New York City, which at the time was a prominent manufacturer of brass and iron ornamental ware.

Although weather vanes designed by Teddy Tiffin are not as old as the full-bodied copper vanes sought by collectors today, a vane designed by this master artist should certainly be considered collectible. While they do not exhibit the primitive charm of some of the older weather vanes or the elaborate detail of the late nineteenth-century weather vanes that are currently bringing such high prices, their refinement of style and their themes make them an echo of what might be called the F. Scott Fitzgerald period in this country's history.

The silhouette weather vanes of genre scenes, rich men's hobbies and sports, and subjects of American regional interest are truly collector's items of the future and should be considered with respect by anyone interested in the history of American folk art. They were a successful attempt on the part of the designers and manufacturers to present to the public weather vanes of subjects that would appeal to Americans in all parts of the country at prices that most home-owners could afford. Many of these vanes are so graceful that it is difficult to believe that they were cut from rather thick metal.

The success of the leading weather-vane manufacturers in reviving for a time an ancient art form with delicate detailing that could stand up to any climatic conditions is certainly important to the total picture of American weather-vane production. To reproduce a small-scaled engine or horse or other subject in three dimensions took great skill on the part of the nineteenth-century craftsmen. The success of the later silhouette weather vanes required the designs of talented artists who were able to simplify their subjects to the point where the outline was all that created the picture.

Kenneth Lynch holding Tiffin-designed
vane, "On the Ball." Lynch silhouette
vanes were copper and usually painted
black. To right of photo is case holding
patterns for silhouette vanes made in
the 1920s and 1930s.

Silhouette vane, "Jouster," made by Kenneth Lynch and Sons, Incorporated. This design is Lynch's trademark.

"Military Jump" by Lynch is thirty inches long.

"March Wind" by Lynch is twenty-seven and a half inches long.

"Don Quixote" silhouette is extremely suitable subject for weather vane. Length: thirty inches. Made by Kenneth Lynch and Sons, Incorporated.

"The Hounds" is Teddy Tiffin's design made by Kenneth Lynch and Sons, Incorporated. Length: twenty-four inches.

"Plowman" is good silhouette design. Made by Kenneth Lynch and Sons, Incorporated. Length: twenty-eight and a half inches.

"Stage Coach" is Lynch silhouette
vane that was made in two sizes,
twenty-two and a half and thirty-two
inches long.

"The Archer" vane is a superb example
of silhouette art found in vanes of
the 1920s and 1930s. Made by Kenneth
Lynch and Sons, Incorporated.
Twenty-four and a half inches long.

"Covered Wagon" vane by Lynch firm.
Length: thirty inches.

"Bucking Broncho" silhouette made to
appeal to western and midwestern
customers of Lynch firm.

"Valkyrie" silhouette was made in two
sizes: twenty and thirty-six inches
long. Made by Kenneth Lynch and
Sons, Incorporated.

"Goose Girl" by Lynch is nicely balanced
design. Twenty-seven and a half
inches long.

"Green Pastures" vane portrays
tranquil cow under a tree. Twenty-six
and a half inches long. Made by
Kenneth Lynch and Sons, Incorporated.

"Old Dobbin" is humorous Lynch
weather vane in silhouette form.
Twenty-one and a half inches long.

"Mary's Lamb," made by Kenneth
Lynch and Sons, Incorporated, is
twenty-eight inches long.

"Three Bears" holding bowls of porridge
is silhouette vane adapted from
children's story. Made by Lynch in
two sizes: eleven and a half and
twenty-two inches long.

"On the Ball" is superb vane design
in silhouette by artist Teddy Tiffin,
made by Kenneth Lynch and Sons,
Incorporated. Tiffin had great feeling of
movement and was master of
foreshortening. Thirty-six inches long.

"Jumper" silhouette vane made by Washburne Company. Made in two sizes: thirty and forty-seven inches long.

"Harried Farmer" is humorous vane made by Lynch firm. Twenty-nine inches long.

"Flying Ducks" by Washburne, like many other silhouette vanes of 1920s, is Art Deco in feeling. Thirty inches long.

"Witch," made by Washburne, is humorous subject made in thirty-six-inch length.

"Farmer" by Washburne is vane that "tells a story." Length: twenty-eight inches.

Witch on broom silhouette on Pomona, home of Mrs. Albert D. Hutzler, Pikesville, Maryland.

Washburne silhouette vane, "Mayflower."
Length: twenty-eight inches.

"Brig Topaz–1807" is historical ship
vane in silhouette made by Washburne.
Length: twenty-two inches.

Intricate silhouette design of pastoral
scene with building is on schoolhouse
in Amenia, New York.

Connecticut's historic tree, "Charter
Oak," is vane on Southbury Training
School, Southbury, Connecticut.

6

COLLECTING
WEATHER VANES

Few of the weather vanes currently being offered for sale by antique dealers can be considered true antiques in terms of the United States Department of Customs interpretation. According to that department's regulations, an article must be at least one hundred years old before it is a genuine antique and therefore not subject to import duties. The weather vanes today's collectors are seeking were all of domestic manufacture and of course would never be dutiable. But the ruling does point up the relative newness of the weather vanes for which high prices are being paid.

Occasionally one will find a true primitive vane of unquestionable provenance and artistic merit. It is curious, however, that these rarely command the biggest price tags. What you will see most often in this type of weather vane is a rusted silhouette of a horse or rooster cut out of thin sheet iron or a crudely carved wood figure, arrow, or banneret device. The difficulty for the dealer in attempting to charge a great deal of money for this kind of vane is that they are terribly difficult to authenticate and extremely simple to duplicate.

Unless there is adequate documentation as to who made the primitive weather vane, when it was made, and where it was situated, as well as the circumstances of its removal, buying these vanes involves a certain degree of risk. Without this information these vanes must be bought strictly for their decorative appeal and not thought of as an investment. It does not require enormous skill for someone today to cut a piece of sheet metal with a pair of tin snips from a pattern copied from the *Index of American Design* or another reference source. There are still whittlers around who can fashion an old piece of lumber into a weather vane that looks as though it has been around for a couple of centuries. If the sweep of the tail feathers on a weathercock is modified just right, the weather vane can be promoted as a previously undiscovered vane made by James Lombard.

It is the factory-made weather vanes that are setting record prices at auctions and for which the dealers are unblushingly asking four- and five-figure prices. Most of these vanes date from the mid- to late nineteenth century, and a great many of them are of considerably later origin. The most desirable weather vanes in this category are those of unusual subjects found in the early catalogs of makers such as Fiske, Cushing, Washburne, and Harris. Even the more common cows, horses, sheep, roosters, and eagles have considerable value if the pattern can be pointed out as being the same as in one of the old catalogs.

From our knowledge of how hollow-body copper weather vanes are made and the craftsmanship that went into their modeling and fabrication, it is fair to value them as minor works of art. But in a country such as ours, hungry for an artistic legacy, these commercially made weather vanes have recently been promoted to the status of a major American folk art. This is not meant to downgrade their importance as an original and often beautiful expression of native arts and crafts but rather to place them in perspective with the truly creative efforts of the individual craftsmen. Their real value is the recognition that these late nineteenth-century weather vanes are a record of the patriotic enthusiasms, the commercial endeavors, and the artistic tastes of that period in our history.

Another consideration concerning the late nineteenth-century weather vanes as collectible objects is that many of the full-bodied elaborate vanes that adorned the stables, barns, and houses of the wealthy merchants and industrialists of the period will never be made again. Although many of the old molds still exist and the weather vanes could be reproduced, architectural styles have changed, and the nineteenth-century vane designs are no longer suitable for modern buildings. Where weather vanes are used to adorn new buildings, contemporary patterns are made for them. Where weather vanes are ordered in traditional designs, prices are necessarily high due to the lack of craftsmen skilled in copper work and gold-leafing.

There is little question that the elaborate copper weather vanes of the late nineteenth century and the first part of this century preceding the Great Depression are worth preserving and collecting. However, it is important for anyone making a major investment in one of these vanes to realize what period of American art and architecture they represent. It would also be helpful for the collector to know that certain of these designs have been continuously made to the present day. Many of these vanes are made as antique reproductions and are represented as such in current catalogs. While most of these modern vanes are being made in aluminum rather than copper and therefore are easier to identify as modern, others are still being produced in copper, and as time goes on, these will be more difficult to detect as being recent, especially those that are produced from the old molds.

Interestingly, the vanes of patriotic nature have been commanding the highest prices on the current market. The eagle, the figure of the Goddess of Liberty, "Liberty Enlightening the World," which is a copy of the Statue of Liberty, and the Liberty Cap vane all seem to be in demand. While some of these vanes have a primitive appearance, all of these motifs were used in the late nineteenth century.

Weather vanes that are miniature sculptures of the elaborate vehicles of the late nineteenth and early twentieth centuries have recently gained a great deal of popularity with collectors. The steam fire engine, hook and ladder, and locomotive and tender all have the appearance of made-to-scale copper toys, and a great deal of attention was given to realism of detail in the design and execution of these vanes. They would cost thousands of dollars to reproduce today.

Locomotives and tenders adorned the railway stations of the period, and these elaborate vanes, expensive to begin with, are eagerly sought by railway buffs. The importance of the river steamer and ferry boat to midwesterners in the nineteenth century caused the design of several vanes in these motifs, and again, these are perfect replicas and important documents of American history. All of these weather vanes are recorded in the Fiske Company catalog of 1893.

At the beginning of this century, as the horseless carriages replaced horse-drawn vehicles, model automobiles were used as motifs for weather vanes. E. G. Washburne made several models of open touring cars in gilded copper. During the pre-Depression days of great affluence these vanes adorned the garages of the rich in the same manner that the horse vanes were used on stables. Full-bodied sailboats, trotting horses and carts, horses with jockeys, and hounds chasing deer were other weather vanes that represented the hobbies of the wealthy class.

The collector should keep in mind, however, that the more traditional motifs of cows, roosters, fish, and horses were used in quantity in the late nineteenth century and were continued in production throughout the first quarter of this century. Elaborate bannerets were also used in profusion during the period under discussion, and while these seem to be in less demand today by collectors than the full-bodied models of animals, automobiles, engines, and other types of vanes, many of them required complicated handwork in their manufacture and should not be overlooked.

The late nineteenth century was a period when there was a great deal of interest in the fauna of other lands and although domestic animal subjects such as pigs, roosters, horses, and cows were still in demand as weather-vane motifs, ostriches, elephants, lions, and boars shared the American skyline. Mythological dragons were also a turn-of-the-century subject that was utilized by the weather-vane manufacturers. These were especially involved figures to make in full-bodied copper weather vanes.

The collector should also keep in mind that although the elaborate copper weather vanes with gold-leafing are typical of the latter part of the nineteenth century, many of these were quite expensive when new, and home craftsmen across the United States continued to make their own weather vanes in the eighteenth- and early nineteenth-century tradition and motifs. As has already been pointed out, simple silhouette weather vanes are not difficult to make and could be just as functional, if not quite as decorative, as the full-bodied copper figure of Mercury or a gilded eagle with a two-foot wingspread. When these later handmade weather vanes appear on the antiques market, they are usually impossible to date, and dealers tend to call all weather vanes of his type late nineteenth century. Some claim that they are even older.

The collector might well ask if it is possible that some of the late nineteenth- and early twentieth-century weather vanes currently being offered for sale are really recent reproductions. Can a reproduction be made to duplicate old catalog patterns and give evidence of years of exposure to the elements? The answer is definitely yes.

It must first be realized that the nineteenth-century manufacturers studiously copied each other's designs. Some of the renderings of classic subjects such as famous trotting horses, prize cattle, or patriotic motifs are practically identical from maker to maker. So much so, in fact, that it would lead us to believe that the old companies made castings of each other's products and incorporated them into their lines. Thus it proves difficult in many cases to attribute positively a horse and sulky vane to Cushing, Fiske, Washburne, or someone else. Reference to catalog drawings are not always conclusive, because these are artist's sketches and not photographs of the actual weather vane. In production the harness on a trotting horse may be placed differently from the catalog illustration or other details in the drawings were not able to be reproduced faithfully in the copper.

It must also be remembered that the iron molds from which these vanes were made are almost indestructible. An article appeared in *Time* magazine in 1954 concerning the discovery by the late Edith Halpert of a valuable cache of old molds the previous year. Mrs.

Halpert, a gallery owner, collector, and expert on American folk art, was convinced that some old molds must still be in existence. After searching the East Coast area for ten years, she finally found "a jumble of 350 Cushing molds in the yard of a Chelsea, Massachusetts, junkman." Under her supervision sixteen new weather vanes were made from the old molds and placed on exhibition in the American Artists Galleries in New York. Up to twenty copies of each weather vane were reproduced and offered for sale at prices up to five hundred dollars. The molds now are part of the collection of the American Museum of Folk Art in New York City.

The fact that these Cushing molds are now out of circulation does not mean that there are no other old molds still being worked. To the contrary, weather vanes are still being produced from Washburne molds in Danvers, Massachusetts, and from Fiske molds in Brooklyn, New York. No doubt there are other nineteenth-century molds in use elsewhere. A manufacturer with access to these molds has stated that some of his best customers are antique dealers.

The only problem an antique dealer has once he secures a new weather vane made from an old mold is in ageing the vane. While it is true that few antique dealers would go to the lengths required to age a new weather vane in order to pass it off as an old one, this practice does exist, and the collector should be aware of it.

Ageing a new weather vane by artificial means does require patience, attention to detail, and a little knowledge of chemistry. Copper can be blackened to resemble exposure to years of chimney soot and other air pollutants by treating it with potassium sulphide, sometimes called liver of sulphate. The inside of the vane in particular must be treated with this compound in order for it to pass close scrutiny.

The process involves one or two small holes first being drilled in the bottom of the vane. The potassium sulphide is then introduced, sloshed around, and emptied. The holes are either filled in or left as weep holes for the moisture (caused by condensation) to escape. Providing weep holes was a fairly common practice in weather-vane construction, so the presence of these in a weather vane is not necessarily evidence of artificial ageing.

The acquisition of the typical greenish patina of copper can be accelerated by treating it with copper sulphate and acetic acid. A better but more time-consuming method involves burying a new vane for three or four months. In this procedure the weather vane is placed in a box large enough to contain it, and the bottom of it is covered with ordinary dirt. Next, the vane is covered with any kind of animal manure. The box is then filled with dirt and buried in the ground. During the time the box is underground the contents are kept damp by the application of salt water. After the vane is removed from this compost, it has a mottled, random patina that looks quite genuine. If the vane still doesn't look quite old enough and seems to require additional treatment, it is kept in a pan and from time to time chemicals are dripped over it the same way one would baste a turkey.

Prior to the chemical treatment a thoughtful forger must apply a few artistic touches of his own. It is well known that few farm boys could resist trying out their new .22 rifles or BB guns on the weather vane on top of the old barn. Weather vanes make marvelous targets. When you hit them, they spin around with a very satisfying action. That is why so many of the old vanes now on sale bear the dents and holes inflicted by generations of small boys plinking away at them. So to complete the aura of age, a new vane that is going to be sold as "antique" must also become a target and be shot at a few times in noncritical areas of its anatomy. It would not do to shoot off a head, foot, or tail and thus seriously reduce a weather vane's value.

The above detailed description is certainly not meant to be a "how to" for the few unscrupulous antique dealers who may not have known how to age new weather vanes before reading it. It is merely given as a warning to collectors and would-be collectors to prevent their purchasing a new, doctored weather vane at the high prices presently being asked for genuine old ones. Whenever prices become high enough in any category of collecting, there will always be some attempts to reproduce the collected objects. If the collector buys vanes only from established, reputable antique dealers, there should be no problem.

7

BANNERS, BANNERETS,
AND ARROWS

Banners or pennants were two of the earliest motifs of weather vanes and have also been the most persistent. With origins in dim medieval history, the banner or pennant that a knight or noble was permitted to display on his castle made the transition from cloth to more durable metal at least five hundred years ago. Examples from the fourteenth and fifteenth centuries are still preserved on buildings and in museums on the European continent and in Great Britain.

The first of these banner vanes were made without arrows· or other pointing devices in front of the representation of the flag. Later, they were embellished with additional ironwork that provided ornamentation in front of the banner and was the part that pointed into the wind. The traditional banner vane was carried to the New World, and its manufacture here departed very little from the European custom until the eighteenth century.

One of the most striking American modifications of the banner or banneret weather vane was the incorporation of the arrow into the design. The Americans first appended arrowheads on the front of their banner vanes and then added the tail feathers as well. The design of the banners became freer, and other motifs crept in and were combined with the basic arrow form. Some of these shapes were the lyre, star, heart, scroll, and flower. Variations on these themes were endless, and they were worked and reworked by a lot of the weather-vane manufacturers as well as local blacksmiths, wood-carvers, and amateur craftsmen.

The basic guidelines for the design of banneret weather vanes were laid down by the leading architects of the seventeenth and eighteenth centuries. In England Sir Christopher Wren and James Gibbs adapted the strict heraldic banners of the Gothic to the steepled churches and public buildings they were designing. Their influence carried over to the American colonies, and their ideas influenced Shem Drowne's banneret vane for Old North Church and the later work of Charles Bullfinch, Asher Benjamin, and even Thomas Jefferson.

Jefferson and Benjamin strove for the greater purity and simplicity of line that was part of the classic revival in the period from 1790 to 1820. During this time Benjamin wrote several books on architectural practice which had a profound influence on contemporary builders and designers. Prior to his treatises, *Practice of Architecture* and *Country Builder's Assistant*, the man who built a building was generally its designer as well. These builders eagerly copied and adapted Benjamin's designs to the town halls, churches, and homes they were then constructing. Copies of Benjamin's weather-vane designs can still be found on churches and public buildings in Massachusetts and Vermont.

Weather vanes designed by Thomas Jefferson are shown in some still preserved fragments of his drawings and on buildings at the University of Virginia. Of course, Jefferson's best known weather vane can still be seen on top of his home in Monticello. The Monticello weather vane was unique for its time in that the shaft led down from the roof to an indicator in the ceiling of the room beneath it. In that way one could tell the direction of the wind without going outside or looking out a window. This feature was particularly useful at night.

Aside from the plain, ordinary arrow weather vanes, the banneret type has the widest geographical distribution in the United States. It would appear that outside of the northeastern part of the country architects' tastes were quite conservative. On churches, homes, and public buildings the banneret was often chosen. This was true in the South as early as 1714, as shown in the unusual plantation home known as Mulberry in South Carolina which is located about forty miles northwest of Charleston. This brick edifice has four round towers located at each corner. On top of each of these turrets is an iron banner vane with the date 1714 pierced in each one.

There are other surviving examples of restorations of buildings of colonial America exhibiting banneret weather vanes. The Williamsburg restoration has traditional bannerets on the Governor's Palace and on the Court House. Independence Hall in Philadelphia is another important eighteenth-century building with a banneret weather vane.

Bannerets are also the most frequently seen vane motif in the Midwest and Northwest. On the farms in the prairie states farmers depended upon the windmills used to pump water to learn from which direction the wind was blowing. In the towns bannerets and arrows were the vane motifs most commonly in use. These were, in the case of the more ambitious ones, ordered from one of the eastern manufacturers through a local hardware store or directly by mail.

In the late nineteenth century the rich were building elaborately decorated homes in the Gothic and Greek revival styles as well as imitations of Italian villas and French châteaus. Where the design of these houses lent itself to the use of weather vanes, they called for bannerets to complete the Old World baronial image. A weather vane would have spoiled the symmetry of the flat-topped Italianate towers but were suitable for the round pointed peaks on the turrets of the Gothic style houses. However, finials of wood or iron are more often found on these Victorian turrets than weather vanes. Many of these were supplied by weather-vane manufacturers.

In the Southwest the Spanish mission style of architecture with its long low lines did not encourage the use of weather vanes for decorative purposes. This was true also of the equally long and flat prairie style buildings of the Midwest as promulgated by Frank Lloyd Wright around the beginning of this century. The only house designed by Wright with a weather vane appears to be one built for a member of the Johnson (wax manufacturing) family in Racine, Wisconsin. It is not known whether the plain arrow vane was part of Wright's original plan or if it was a later addition.

The châteaus built by the very rich at Newport, Rhode Island, and George Washington Vanderbilt's country residence, Biltmore, in Asheville, North Carolina, have discreet banner weather vanes at their peaks. Their architects, principally H. H. Richardson and R. M. Hunt, seemed not to place any undue emphasis on the originality of the vanes that topped these imposing edifices and apparently were satisfied to order stock patterns. Vanes of this kind would be valuable from a collector's standpoint, not for any distinction of the weather-vane design itself but for the associations with the building from which it had been removed.

Banners, bannerets, and arrows as a category of collectible weather vanes have been relatively neglected up to this time. They should become more desirable and their value increase as fewer of the genuinely old figural and genre vanes come onto the market. A graceful, well-made banneret vane, particularly if it is from a local landmark, will make a handsome wall decoration that has a historical association as well.

Wrought iron weather vanes on each of
four corner turrets of plantation house,
Mulberry, in South Carolina. Each
vane has the date 1714 pierced into it.

Banneret weather vane on Independence
Hall, Philadelphia, Pennsylvania.

Detail from architectural drawing by
Thomas Jefferson of cupola showing
weather-vane design.

Three drawings by Asher Benjamin, one of America's first important architects, showing use of banneret-arrow vanes.

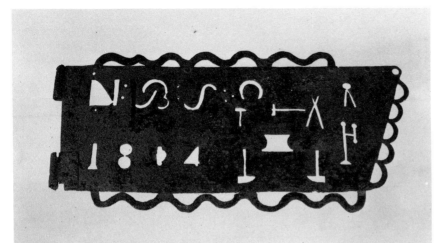

Blacksmith weather vane, 1804 or 1814,
made of sheet iron. Nine and a half
inches high by twenty inches long.
(*Shelburne Museum*)

Banneret vane on United Church, the
Green, New Haven, Connecticut.

Early nineteenth-century iron arrow vane
on abandoned meeting house in South
Britain, Connecticut.

Bannerets were often personalized with owner's initials. North Adams, Massachusetts.

Arrow piercing an apple is mid-nineteenth-century vane found in Maine. Length: fifty inches. (*Gary Cole*)

The library in De Pere, Wisconsin, has stylized arrow vane.

59

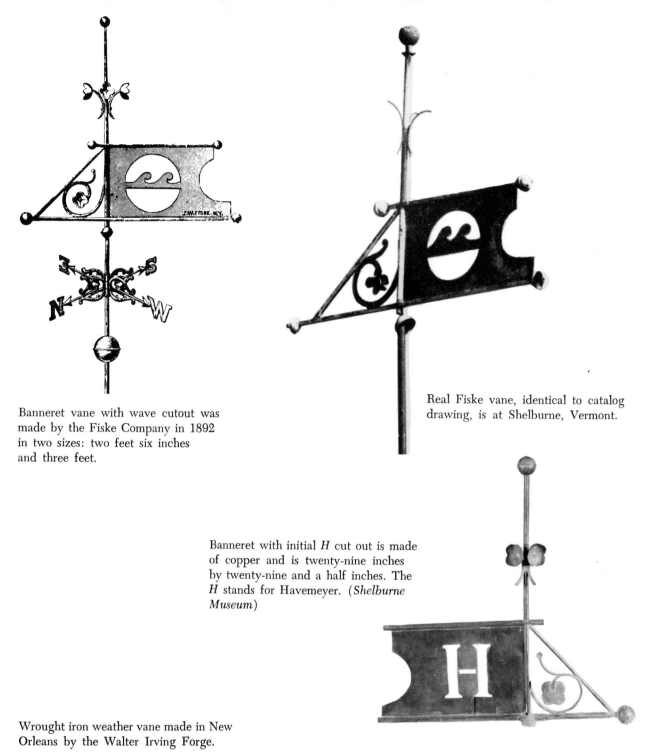

Banneret vane with wave cutout was made by the Fiske Company in 1892 in two sizes: two feet six inches and three feet.

Real Fiske vane, identical to catalog drawing, is at Shelburne, Vermont.

Banneret with initial *H* cut out is made of copper and is twenty-nine inches by twenty-nine and a half inches. The *H* stands for Havemeyer. (*Shelburne Museum*)

Wrought iron weather vane made in New Orleans by the Walter Irving Forge.

Banneret vane on the Governor's Palace in Williamsburg, Virginia

Banneret with star at top is on Episcopal Church in Bethany, Connecticut.

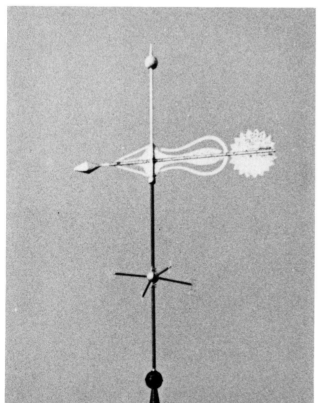

Banneret with star at end is on church in Litchfield, Connecticut.

Banneret on church in Roxbury, Connecticut

Church banneret of local make in Northfield, Vermont

Copy of Shem Drowne Old North
Church vane is on church in
Williamstown, Massachusetts.

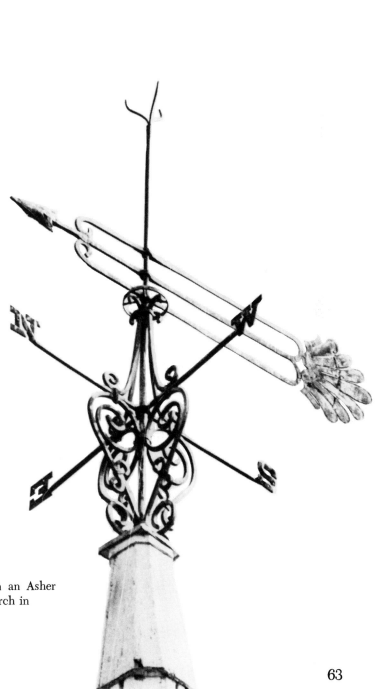

Banneret–arrow vane from an Asher
Benjamin design is on church in
Northfield, Vermont.

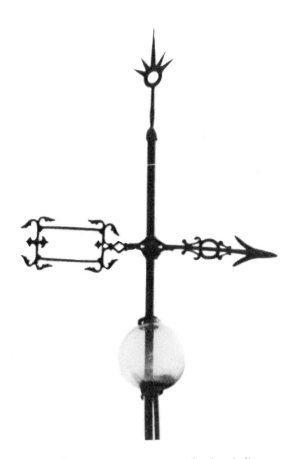

Banneret–arrow vane with glass ball on shaft is on barn in East Braintree, Vermont. Vane is also lightning rod.

Banneret vane on Congregational Church in Randolph, Vermont

Gilded copper arrow vane of latter half of nineteenth century is on store in Shelburne, Vermont.

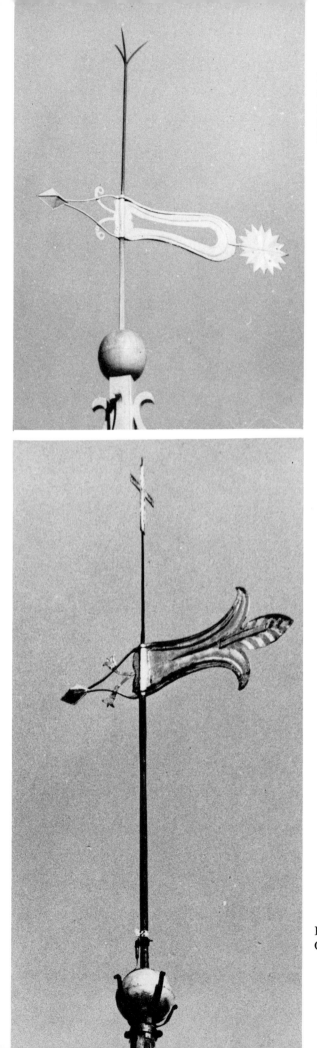

Banneret with star is on United Church of Christ in Bethany, Connecticut. It closely resembles other church vanes in the area, and all were probably made by the same maker.

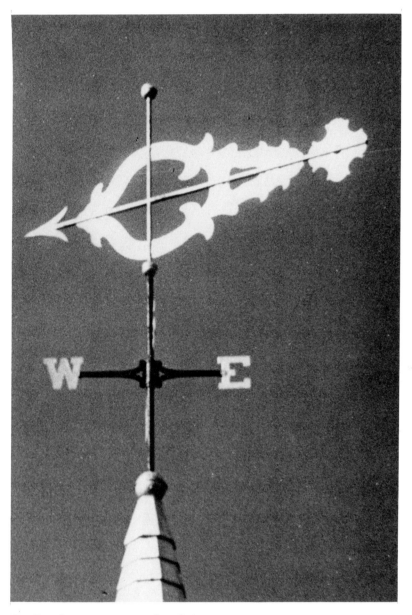

Scroll and arrow vane on church in Harwinton, Connecticut, can be identified as having been made by the Washburne Company. Washburne's cardinal points are distinctive.

Banneret with cross on Congregational Church in Norfolk, Connecticut

65

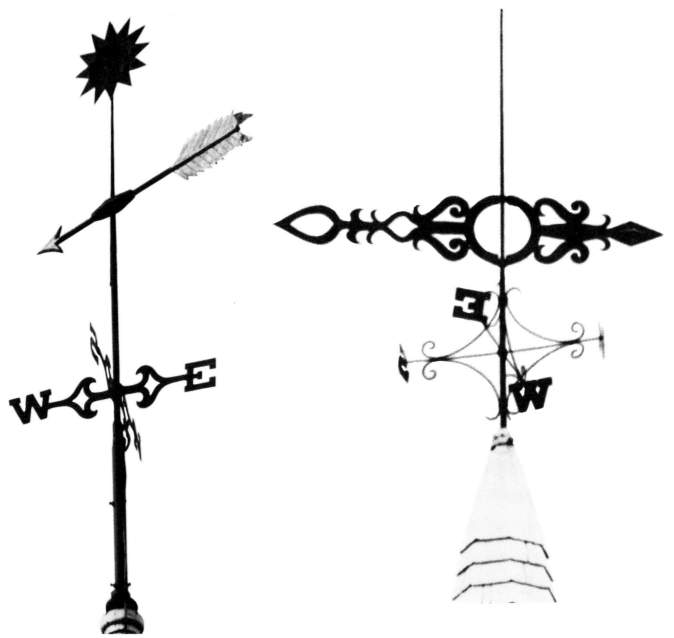

Arrow with star vane can be identified by the cardinal points as having been made by Cushing Company.

Handsome arrow vane is on church in South Randolph, Vermont.

Banneret–arrow vane with two stars in on North Congregational Church in Woodbury, Connecticut. Church was built in 1817.

Arrow with intricate scrollwork on church in Williamstown, Vermont

The First Congregational Church in Woodbury, Connecticut, also has a handsome banneret vane with piercing to vary the design.

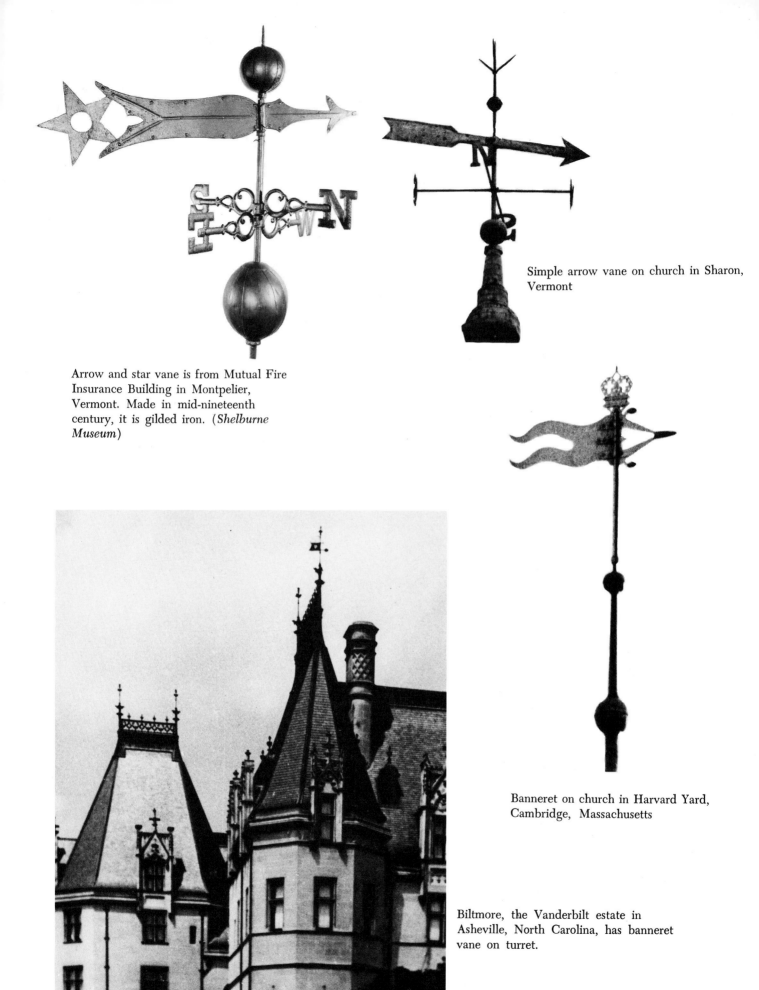

Arrow and star vane is from Mutual Fire Insurance Building in Montpelier, Vermont. Made in mid-nineteenth century, it is gilded iron. (*Shelburne Museum*)

Simple arrow vane on church in Sharon, Vermont

Banneret on church in Harvard Yard, Cambridge, Massachusetts

Biltmore, the Vanderbilt estate in Asheville, North Carolina, has banneret vane on turret.

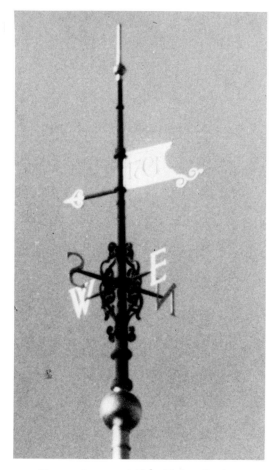

Banneret vane at Yale University in New Haven, Connecticut, has date 1931 pierced into it.

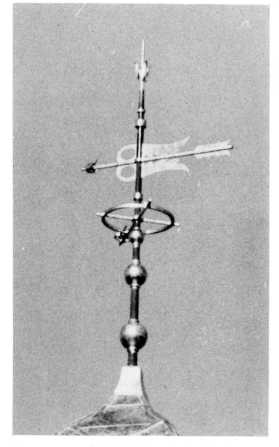

Banneret vane at Yale University is close replica of vane on Independence Hall in Philadelphia.

Banneret vane at Yale with date countersunk into it

69

Yale University's motto, "Light and
Truth," inscribed in Hebrew in wrought
iron vane on one of school's buildings.

Arrow vane on Maryland Casualty
Insurance Company in Baltimore,
Maryland, is company's trademark.

Intricately pierced banneret vane on City
Hall in Waterbury, Connecticut, is
early twentieth century.

Weather vane of banneret shape was
on steeple of First Methodist Church in
Waterbury, Connecticut, which was
built in 1870 and torn down in 1972.

70

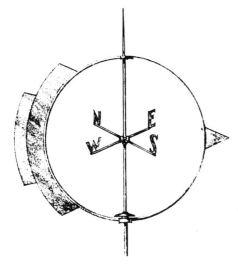

Banneret–arrow vane made in 1956 in antique style is on Williamstown Savings Bank in Williamstown, Massachusetts.

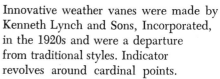

Innovative weather vanes were made by Kenneth Lynch and Sons, Incorporated, in the 1920s and were a departure from traditional styles. Indicator revolves around cardinal points.

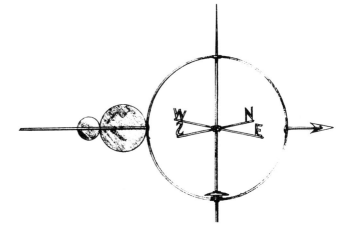

Vanes made by the Lynch firm in the 1930s were in Art Deco style and were not commercially successful. They are collector's items today.

E. G. Washburne Company advertised this electric weather vane, which could be read indoors, in their catalog in the 1920s.

71

8

WEATHERCOCKS

It has already been established that the rooster gained its great popularity as a subject for weather vanes through the Papal decree that proclaimed it as a symbol of the betrayal of Christ, reminding all Christians not to repeat this sin. The rooster also reminded the faithful that their first obligation in the morning was to pray. While the use of the rooster as a religious symbol for vanes can be traced as far back as the ninth century in Catholicism, it also became a decoration on non-Catholic church spires when other sects of Christianity became established. For many years the word "weathercock" has been synonymous with "weather vane."

In a nonreligious sense the rooster or cock played an important part in ancient cultures, where it was bred for fighting purposes. Ancient Chinese records indicate that cockfighting was popular in the Orient, and the Greeks and Romans are known to have bet large sums of money on their favorite fighters. Cockfighting in England was practiced as early as the thirteenth century, and it was not until the nineteenth century that laws were passed prohibiting cockfighting in Great Britain, Canada, and parts of the United States. This sport is still carried on in various parts of the world.

Throughout the history of literature the cock is the proud announcer of time and the advent of the dawn of a new day. It is also a symbol of pride. Chaucer told of the proud cock in his *Nun's Priest's Tale*. Chanticleer is described in this story as being a teller of time "more trusty . . . than a clock or an abbey horologe; he knew by nature each revolution of the equictial in that longitude, for when each fifteen degrees were ascended, then he crew, that it could not be bettered."

Time and the weather have always been elements that govern men's lives. The rooster, which made the first sound of the day, seemed a fitting motif for a weather vane.

Most religious symbols were born in pagan lore, and it is probable that the rooster is no exception. Certainly, Freudian psychologists would find many pertinent reasons why the cock became the most popular weather indicator and has decorated spires and cupolas from early times. The fighting rooster is the ideal symbol of masculine strength. It is a virile, polygamous animal that rules the barnyard and can happily care for a dozen or more hens. Even Chaucer's Chanticleer, whose romantic interest was the Demoiselle Partlet, "had in his governance seven hens, to do all his pleasure."

There are, of course, other reasons why the rooster became the most popular motif for weather vanes. Perhaps the most simple non-religious and non-Freudian explanation is that the profile shape of the bird is ideal as a vane, for it has direction, windfoil, and perfect balance. The arched tail feathers and the regal comb would be simplified by the early artisan to present from a distance a recognizable figure that, once mounted, would swing freely with the wind. Because the rooster was a common bird, one could easily recognize the form when it was perched on the highest steeple or rooftop in town.

Through many centuries the cock was given the job of predicting wind direction more often than any other vane motif. His popularity as a weather vane only began to wane in the nineteenth century, when roosters and hens were bred for food rather than breeding the male as a fighter. Many of the earliest American weathercocks that still survive are legless, two-dimensional, and highly stylized. By the mid-nineteenth century more realistic weathercocks were made in full-bodied copper figures.

If the basic shape of the rooster used as an American weather-vane motif seemed to have changed over the years, it is because real roosters changed shape as they were crossbred. The British rooster vanes are representative of the Cornish chickens that were brought to America and crossbred with Mediterranean strains. This produced an American breed of poultry in which the male had highly arched tail feathers and an elegance of shape not found in its European ancestors.

Important early weathercocks can still be found performing their original function on steeples and rooftops throughout New England. The most significant of these is the aforementioned Shem Drowne rooster on the steeple of The First Church in Cambridge, Massachusetts. Drowne's rooster was made originally for the New Brick Church in Boston in 1721 which was built by a secessionist group. Weighing 172 pounds and over five feet tall, Drowne's rooster was made of copper and, like Drowne's famous grasshopper, has a glass eye. It has an open beak and high comb and, unlike many of the more primitive rooster vanes of the eighteenth century, Drowne's rooster is not legless and exhibits the sharp spurs of the fighting cock.

While the New England skyline is still rampant with rooster weather vanes, some of which date from the eighteenth century, others can be found in the Hudson River Valley region of New York. The earliest recorded rooster vane in the United States still in use adorns the First Church in Albany, New York. This vane was brought from Holland in 1656. It is these early imported vanes that came from Holland and England that continued to make the motif popular with American weather-vane makers.

As Americans settled further and further west, they brought with them their traditions and architectural styles, and rooster shapes of the late eighteenth and early nineteenth centuries moved west also. While rooster vanes of this period cannot be found in great numbers in areas outside of New England, New York, and Pennsylvania, later ones do exist in other parts of the United States.

One of the most interesting and complete collections of early rooster weather vanes can be seen at the Shelburne Museum in Vermont. A handsome eighteenth-century vane in that collection, made of painted wood and iron, is a superb example of the simplification of form and stylization typical of the early handmade weathercocks. The head is extremely small in comparison to the body and tail of the bird, and balance is accomplished by the design of a full breast thrust forward and feet that reach forward to the ball on which they are mounted.

Another unusual rooster vane is made of brass and is also highly stylized with only ridges to indicate tail and wing feathers. The various parts of this vane are meticulously riveted together. A more elaborate gamecock is made of two sheets of copper elaborately chiseled to represent feathers. This vane was probably made during the mid-nineteenth century in Connecticut. It was gilded at the time it was made.

A perky weathercock that came from Springfield, Massachusetts, is made of brass with the two sheets hammered and soldered together to form a round-bodied figure. This weathercock dates from around 1800. An interesting pair of weather vanes, obviously taken from the same building, include a large rooster and a smaller hen. Both are mounted on pineapple-shaped wooden finials and are made of polychrome sheet iron. Other rooster vanes in the Shelburne collection include simple primitive wood carvings as well as the later nineteenth-century full-bodied gilded copper roosters.

The rooster began to lose some of his popularity as a weather-vane motif by the middle of the nineteenth century. With the building of the great and elaborate Victorian houses and the diversity of interests of their builders, designers, and architects, weather vanes were made that were more personal symbols of the homeowners or that were more suitable to the eclectic styles of the period. The religious symbolism of the rooster was also forgotten, and church spires were topped off with elaborate bannerets that looked handsome but had no real religious significance.

Even though the weathercock lost some of its popularity as a vane motif by 1850, he was by no means forsaken completely, and the weather-vane manufacturers continued to design and make full-bodied gilded birds with highly realistic features. The rooster as a weather-vane motif is still being used, and new vanes are currently being produced in this everlastingly popular shape.

Earliest weather vane in America. Weathercock on First Church in Albany, New York. Brought from Holland in 1656, originally for the Dutch Reformed Church in Albany. Recently made duplicate is now installed on church with original on display inside. Copper and brass.

Shem Drowne copper rooster with glass
eyes is five feet tall. It was made in
1722 and is now on First Church in
Cambridge, Massachusetts.

Gamecock from Springfield,
Massachusetts. Made around 1800.
(*Shelburne Museum*)

Eighteenth-century rooster from Fitch
Tavern, Concord, Massachusetts.
Painted wood and tin. Length: forty-five
inches; height: thirty-four and
a half inches. (*Shelburne Museum*)

Sheet-iron rooster vane, nineteenth
century, originally from Pennsylvania
(*Frank Ganci*)

Rooster attributed to James Lombard,
Baldwin, Maine. Nineteenth-century
wood carving. Length: twenty inches;
height: sixteen inches. (*Shelburne
Museum*)

Rooster vane, New England, carved
from one piece of wood with metal
reinforcing strips (*Shelburne Museum*)

Rooster vane. Wood reinforced with
metal strips. Early nineteenth century.
(*Shelburne Museum*)

Miniature rooster weather vane.
Handmade in early nineteenth century.
Copper. Length: twelve inches.

Rooster vane made of sheet brass,
riveted together. Length: thirty-two
inches; height: twenty-seven inches.
(*Shelburne Museum*)

Rooster weather vane, found in
Pennsylvania. Early nineteenth century.
Wood carving painted black with red
comb. Length: thirty inches; height:
twenty-two inches. (*Shelburne Museum*)

Rooster vane with hand of God symbol.
Found in Pennsylvania. Cut iron,
painted. Height: thirty-three inches.
(*Shelburne Museum*)

Rooster vane "Le Coq de Gallas" from
Burgundy, France, was made in 1636.
It is sheet metal, tin, and wings were
added separately. Length: twenty-one
and a half inches; height: twenty-three
inches. (*Shelburne Museum*)

Rooster vane, early nineteenth century.
Found in Pennsylvania. Gilded copper.
Length: eighteen inches; height:
seventeen inches. (*Shelburne Museum*)

Rooster, originally a weather vane, rests on barn ventilator. Made around 1850. Length: twenty-five inches. (*Shelburne Museum*)

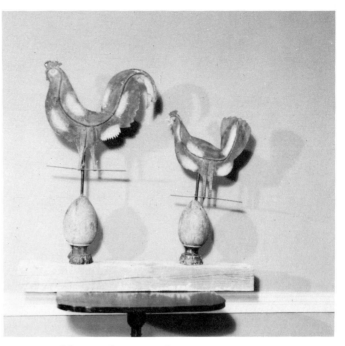

Rooster and hen, mid-nineteenth century. Sheet iron, polychromed. (*Shelburne Museum*)

Crowing cock. Painted iron. Found in Massachusetts. Length: twenty and a half inches; height: nineteen inches. (*Shelburne Museum*)

Rooster made of cast and sheet iron. Second half of nineteenth century. Length: thirty-six inches; height: thirty-three inches. (*Shelburne Museum*)

Strutting cock, copper with lead feet, from New Hampshire. Height: twenty-four and a half inches, including ball. (*Shelburne Museum*)

Gamecock, late nineteenth century. Painted copper. (*Shelburne Museum*)

Gamecock, gilded copper. Found in Connecticut. Late nineteenth century. Length: thirty-three and a half inches; height: thirty-seven inches. (*Shelburne Museum*)

Rooster vane made of sheet copper in second half of nineteenth century. Length: twelve inches; height: twelve inches. (*Shelburne Museum*)

82

The New York Post Office, as seen
in 1843 engraving, had rooster vane.

Rooster vane in Norfolk, Connecticut,
is made of gilded copper. Late
nineteenth century, made by W. A. Snow.

Rooster, made in last half of nineteenth century, of gilded copper. Length: twenty-seven inches. (*Smithsonian Institution*)

This crowing rooster in silhouette was designed and made by Garrett Thew, father of vane craftsman John Garret Thew. The elder Thew made many silhouette designs in the thirties and forties.

Crowing rooster atop this Vermont steeple was probably made at end of last century.

Rooster vane on arrow as advertised by
Washburne in 1920 catalog

COPPER WEATHER VANES
Gilded with Gold Leaf

Roosters

No. 169	14 inches high, with 18 inch Arrow	$15.00
No. 170	18 inches high, with 24 inch Arrow	20.00
No. 171	24 inches high, with 30 inch Arrow	33.00
No. 172	28 inches high, with 36 inch Arrow	50.00
No. 173	36 inches high, with 48 inch Arrow	63.00
No. 174	18 inches high, without Arrow	15.00
No. 175	24 inches high, without Arrow	20.00
No. 176	28 inches high, without Arrow	35.00
No. 177	36 inches high, without Arrow	50.00

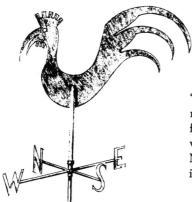

"Coq Fantastique" is antique
reproduction made by Kenneth Lynch
firm around 1935 in iron. Similar
vane was made for guardhouse of
New York State governor's mansion
in 1968.

9

EAGLES AND OTHER
PATRIOTIC VANES

Although American patriotic symbols adorned just about everything produced in this country in the decorative arts following the War of 1812, there are few examples of early weather vanes of patriotic nature surviving today that date prior to the middle of the nineteenth century. The earliest eagle vanes that survive today are simple two-dimensional cutouts made by the amateur craftsman. Other patriotic symbols such as the Goddess of Liberty and the flag were also made, but very few have survived, which suggests they were not made in large quantity. For the first half of the nineteenth century the traditional figure of the rooster that adapted more easily to the silhouette form of vane than the eagle was the more predominant bird motif used. It would take an extremely talented artist to design a flat profile of an eagle so that it would be easily distinguishable from other birds in two dimensions.

The American bald eagle has become an endangered species in recent years, and it is lamentable that few live birds still survive. However, a great many monuments to this bird can be found in the form of weather vanes throughout the country. Almost all of these were made after 1850. These were produced during the period when full-bodied gilded copper vanes were being manufactured. The eagles were made in a great variety of sizes, if not poses, and in their catalog for 1893 the Fiske Company advertises that one of their eagle vanes could be purchased in sizes ranging from a fourteen-foot wingspread to a mere nine inches. These were priced at the time from six hundred dollars for the largest to eight dollars for the smallest.

Although the eagle was not suitable for the techniques of weather-vane making used before 1850, the shape was eminently suitable to the methods of production used after that period. The bird is imposing and realistic when made in full-bodied copper that was gilded. The textured feathers could be reproduced more easily through the use of molds.

There seems to be a great similarity in the various manufacturers' interpretation of the eagle used for weather-vane decoration, and it is often impossible to distinguish among them, even with the use of the various manufacturers' catalogs of the period following 1850. The eagle is always mounted on a ball with his feet together and his wings spread for flight. His head is usually raised and his beak open. Below the ball is an arrow and below that the cardinal points of the compass. While the eagle is always fixed, the arrow indicates the wind direction. As pointed out in an early Washburne catalog, "arrows are indispensable when eagles are used for vanes." There is usually another ball below the cardinal points.

Another patriotic motif weather vane that was also the product of the post-1850 manufacturers is the figure of the Goddess of Liberty. These show the Goddess in her liberty cap holding the American flag in one hand while the other points into the wind. This figure had the proper kind of balance to act as a vane without an arrow, and several manufacturers seem to have used this motif. The subject was obviously not produced in quantity, and when one comes on the market today, it is a widely announced event in the antiques world. Although the figure of the Goddess of Liberty is of late nineteenth-century manufacture, it is in high demand by collectors and museums, and when one is placed on sale, it always brings a very high price.

Another American patriotic symbol that seems to be even more scarce than the figure of the Goddess of Liberty is the vane called Liberty Enlightening the World, which is a replica of the statue erected on Bedloes Island in New York harbor as a gift to the United States by the people of France in 1885. The Statue of Liberty weather vane mounted on an arrow can be found in the Fiske catalog of 1893, but it is probable that other companies also made replicas of this giant statue at the end of the nineteenth century.

Not only the subject of the Statue of Liberty but the material from which the original statue was made would have made the subject especially appealing to the weather-vane manufacturers. Bartholdi's monument is, like the weather vanes of the period, a hollow-bodied copper structure. Interestingly, the vane manufacturers, rather than leave their copper replicas to develop the same green patina as that of the original statue, gold-leafed their copper vanes. Fiske's vane of the statue is three-quarter full-bodied, and there have been versions of the subject found that differ in the turn of the head or other details, probably owing to the various manufacturers' efforts to avoid suits because of copyrights or patents.

Because any weather vane (other than the eagle) made in an American patriotic motif is rarely found today, all vanes of this type are in great demand by museums and private collectors. Any hand-made early nineteenth-century replica of an eagle would be a rarity that should be preserved and recorded. However, for examples of American patriotic symbols made following the War of 1812, when patriotic fervor was at its highest peak in American history, one will have to look elsewhere in the decorative arts. While the proud eagle was a common decoration for plates, jugs, ship prows, and hundreds of other objects, the weathercock still held first place on the steeple.

Eagle made by Boston Metal-Workers Company around 1850. Hand-hammered copper with cast head and feet.

Eagle on arrow weather vane. Copper. Nineteenth century.
(*Shelburne Museum*)

88

Eagle vane on firehouse in Bethel, Vermont, can be identified by cardinal points as having been made by the Snow firm.

Fiske catalog for 1893 shows several eagle vane shapes. The arrow is the vane, and the eagle is fixed on pole.

Eagle on weather vane of Burns Building in Oakville, Connecticut, has graceful wingspread.

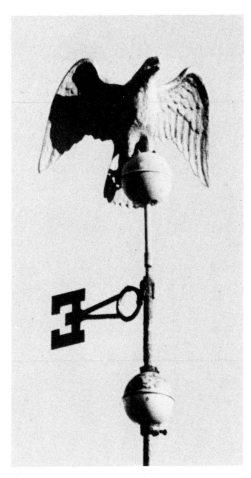

Eagle weather vane on barn in Roxbury, Connecticut

Eagle weather vane on flagpole in center of Amagansett, Long Island. Made by Washburne around 1920.

COPPER WEATHER VANES
Gilded with Gold Leaf

Eagles
ARROWS ARE INDISPENSIBLE
WHEN EAGLES ARE USED FOR VANES

	Spread	Eagle with Arrow, Spire, Letters and Balls	Eagle only on Rod		Spread	Eagle with Arrow, Spire, Letters and Balls	Eagle only on Rod
No. 70	8"	$10.00	$8.00	No. 76	3' 6"	$63.00	$50.00
No. 70A	1' 0"	14.00	11.00	No. 77	4' 0"	90.00	75.00
No. 71	1' 3"	19.00	15.00	No. 78	4' 6"	125.00	88.00
No. 72	1' 6"	27.00	19.00	No. 79	5' 0"	170.00	140.00
No. 73	2' 0"	32.00	25.00	No. 80	5' 6"	190.00	155.00
No. 74	2' 6"	45.00	38.00	No. 81	6' 6"	230.00	188.00
No. 75	3' 0"	57.00	46.00				

Eagle weather vane from Washburne catalog published around 1920. Note cardinal points are same as those on Amagansett eagle vane.

"Goddess of Liberty" weather vane as advertised in 1893 Fiske Company catalog. It was made in two sizes: twenty-four and thirty-six inches high.

Liberty weather vane made by Boston Metal Workers around 1850. Hand-hammered copper. Flag missing.

"Goddess of Liberty" made by Cushing and White around 1865. Copper and zinc, painted and gilded. (*Smithsonian Institution*)

92

Engraving of "Liberty Enlightening the World" weather vane from Fiske catalog of 1893

Rare Goddess of Liberty weather vane with flag and fasces. Length: thirty-seven and a half inches; height: thirty-nine and a half inches. (*Gary C. Cole*)

Statue of Liberty vane. Copper, gilded, made around 1890. Height of figure: forty-seven and a half inches. Length of arrow: fifty-six inches. (*Gerald Kornblau*)

Goddess of Liberty vane. Hammered copper with brass pipe and cast brass eagle on flag staff. Advertised by Cushing from 1865 to 1883. (*Shelburne Museum*)

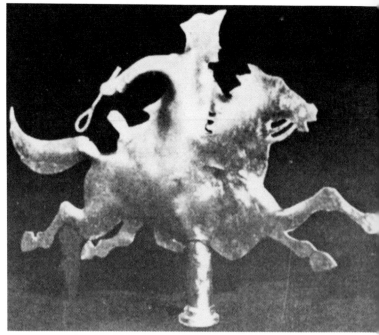

Modern wrought aluminum weather vane
of Paul Revere and his horse. Gilded.
Made for Americana Hotel Systems
in 1965 by Kenneth Lynch and Sons,
Incorporated.

Handmade "Uncle Sam" weather vane.
Painted sheet iron. Nineteenth century.
Found in Connecticut. Height: forty-one
and a half inches. (*Gary C. Cole*)

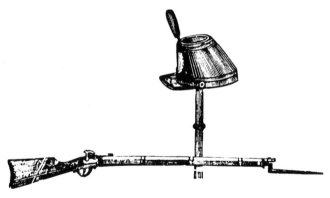

Gun and Cap vane, made in five- or
six-foot lengths. From Fiske catalog
of 1893.

Cannon weather vane. From Fiske
catalog of 1893. Two lengths:
twenty inches or thirty inches.

10

HORSES TO HORSELESS CARRIAGES

If twentieth-century Americans are said to be having a love affair with the automobile, Americans of the nineteenth century had an equal passion for the horse. The horse provided transportation, a means of making a living, sport, and recreation. A good horse was as much a status symbol in the nineteenth century as one of today's expensive sports cars or limousines. As difficult as it is to imagine what our lives would be like without the automobile or truck, it's just as impossible to contemplate life a century or more ago without the horse.

It is not surprising, therefore, to find that horses have been one of the most numerous and persistent subjects of American folk art. Songs were composed about horses, books and stories were written, and horses were sketched, painted, and sculpted. One of the few spectator sports available to Americans before the relatively recent popularity of baseball, football, basketball, and hockey, was horse racing. A renowned racehorse was as much a popular folk hero as a star quarterback, a no-hit pitcher, or a Miss America. Likenesses of outstanding equine excellence were reproduced in the leading periodicals of the day, and thousands of copies of lithographs of famous horses were made and sold by Currier and Ives and other print-makers.

As subjects for weather vanes, horses were used as early as the eighteenth century in primitive iron or wood vanes. They were relatively simple to fashion in outline form and had an inherent grace, movement, and flow that made them ideal vane subjects. The finest development of the horse weather vanes came from the commercial manufacturers in the mid-nineteenth century. Cushing, Snow, Fiske, Washburne, and others hired talented modelers to reproduce likenesses of classic horses as faithfully as possible.

These artists made many of their models from the popular lithographs of record-holding horses published at that time. Line-for-line similarity can be noted between the rendering in a weather vane of a famous horse and in contemporary Currier and Ives prints of the trotters Dexter, Dutchman, Mac, and Ethan Allen. Horses with attached sulkies, both two- and four-wheeled, were also copied from prints and made into handsome weather vanes that are extremely desirable now.

Less glamorous but equally interesting horses were embodied in the primitive vanes made before the manufactured products. Shelburne Museum has a workhorse vane from New Hampshire made of copper and lead that includes the rod and ball as part of the design. Other less sophisticated but amusing weather vanes with horses at Shelburne are the painted sheet-iron vane of Paul Revere on his famous ride and an eighteenth-century Connecticut sheet-iron vane of Washington on horseback. Cast iron horses in the collection are a piebald horse with a tin tail and a formally posed horse made in two halves that were screwed together. The missing tail on the latter was originally riveted to the body. A possibly unique vane also at Shelburne is the bareback rider perched delicately on a galloping horse. This late nineteenth-century handcrafted vane is made of copper filled with lead and was found in Massachusetts.

Sometimes the amateur weather-vane maker was not quite successful in conveying the spirit of a racing horse. The Shelburne Museum has a sheet-iron vane of a horse attached to a sulky that looks as though the horse is pulling a loaded wagon. Much more dashing are the commercial vanes depicting racing horses. The excitement caused by a match race between two renowned horses can be recaptured from an account of a race between the trotters Mac and Zachary Taylor held in Philadelphia on July 18, 1849. The following is a description of the background and setting of the race from the Currier and Ives print commemorating the event.

It will be recollected by the sporting community that the friends of Zachary Taylor, justly proud of the reputation acquired by their horse in the contest with Gray Eagle in the autumn of 1848, boldly challenged by a printed document, the whole world, in the following spring to produce a champion willing and worthy to compete with him for a division of his well-earned laurels. The consequence of this liberal challenge on the part of Zachary's "backers" was the bringing together of the two noble animals represented in the above print. The assemblage on and about the course was perhaps the largest ever witnessed, numbering fully 50,000 persons, collected not only from our city, but from all the principal cities adjoining, as well as far-off states.

There then follows a detailed recapitulation of the three one-mile heats each won by the challenger, Mac, to dethrone the champion, Zachary Taylor. None of our world's heavyweight matches, Super-bowl football games, or World Series could be expected to generate more interest.

Although weather vanes of racehorses were by far the most popular, the 1893 catalog of J. W. Fiske Company offered a number of vanes depicting horses in more mundane situations. There were horses hitched to wagons, carts, sleighs, and even horse cars. Besides horses shown ridden by jockeys or sulky drivers, ladies and gentlemen were mounted on sedate riding horses.

As the automobile began to displace the horse on the roads and highways, it also began to find a place on weather vanes. Beginning early in the twentieth century, weather-vane makers lavished as much attention to detailing a 1909 Hupmobile as they did in making a four-wheeled racing sulky. Most of the activity in automotive weather vanes seems to have occurred in the decade between 1920 and 1930. Typical of this period is the large, open touring car vane made by E. G. Washburne Company, which also offered a vane representing a two-door sports runabout with a rumble seat. Automotive weather vanes went up around the country over garages and automobile dealer showrooms as horses had on barns and livery stables.

No doubt, weather vanes have been made depicting automobile models later than 1930, but none is known to have appeared in dealers' stocks or in collectors' acquisitions. When and if they do, their value will be substantial due to their scarcity, even though they would be less than forty years old.

Tradition has kept alive the horse motif for weather vanes, and many more horses are shown and sold from present-day catalogs than perhaps any other subject. Automobiles are not popular as weather vanes now, and a modern catalog will rarely offer more than one selection—and that will be a 1920s vintage car.

Because horse weather vanes have been so popular for such a long time, a collector should be especially careful about purchasing one. He should be aware that they are still being made today in hollow-bodied copper in the classic patterns from nineteenth-century molds. Often, purchasing a new horse weather vane directly from the maker is a smaller but wiser investment than purchasing the same vane that has been falsely "aged" by an unscrupulous antique dealer.

In 1971 Kenneth Lynch and Sons was awarded a contract to make an unusually large horse weather vane for the Keeneland Racing Association in Lexington, Kentucky. Before initial design was undertaken, photographs were made from various angles of the clubhouse on which the vane was to be placed. The photographs were studied and sketches made to determine the correct dimensions of the horse in relation to the building. Next, the sculptress, Geraldine Lewis Amendola, of Hopkinton, Massachusetts, was commissioned to make a full-sized, five-foot clay model of the famous racehorse Nashua.

After the model was completed, it was shipped to the Lynch workrooms in Wilton, Connecticut, to be used as a guide in fashioning the copper vane. This vane was completely worked up freehand in the repoussé technique from large copper sheets without the aid of molds. As the pieces were hammered into shape, they were fitted to the clay model to check them for accuracy and configuration. The finished vane was mounted on a four-hundred-pound stainless steel shaft and now proudly dominates the Keeneland racetrack building. This vane, for its weight, size, and artistic fidelity, as well as complexity of manufacture, must be judged along with the finest achievements of the art of weather-vane making.

Workhorse weather vane. Ball is included as part of design. Part of horse behind spindle is copper; front is lead for balance. Made in New Hampshire, nineteenth century. (*Shelburne Museum*)

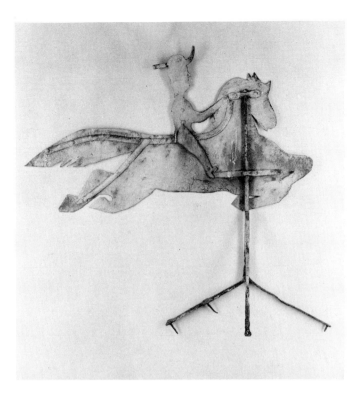

Paul Revere on horseback. Sheet metal painted silver. Length: thirty-six inches. (*Shelburne Museum*)

Washington on horseback. Sheet iron three-sixteenths of an inch thick. Eighteenth century, of Connecticut origin. Length: sixteen and a half inches. (*Shelburne Museum*)

Cast-iron horse in two halves screwed together. Tail missing but was originally riveted to body. Length: twenty-nine inches. (*Shelburne Museum*)

Horse, sheet iron. Exceptionally
graceful sweep of tail and position of
foreleg. Nineteenth century. (*Ryther
House Antiques*)

Horse to sulky. Sheet iron of amateur
design. Found in New Jersey. Nineteenth
century. Length: thirty-six inches.
(*Shelburne Museum*)

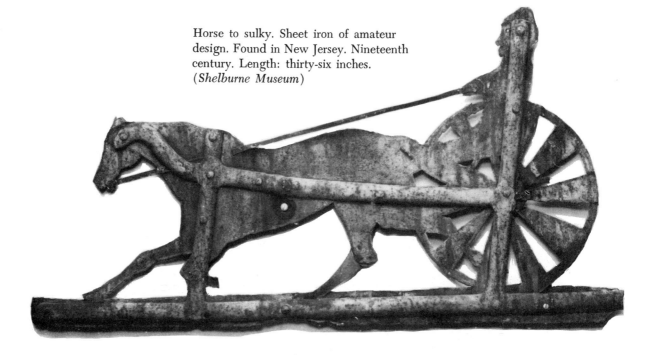

Unusual painted sheet-iron horse with elaborate saddle and harness detail. Handmade.

Piebald horse, cast iron with tin tail. Nineteenth century. (*Shelburne Museum*)

Bareback rider. Copper; lead filled. Found in Massachusetts. Late nineteenth century. Subject for weather vane is unique. Length: thirty and a half inches. (*Shelburne Museum*)

Wood model for horse weather vane. Made in two halves but shown assembled. No vanes made from this mold have been found to date. (*Shelburne Museum*)

Horse vane, copper, half-round. Made around 1850: Length: twenty-three and a half inches. Gift of Annie McKenzie. (*Shelburne Museum*)

Horse vane, sheet iron, is handcrafted version of commercial vanes made in latter half of nineteenth century.

Strongly modeled wood horse weather vane. Nineteenth century. Length: twenty-four inches.

Carousel horse, zinc, made in nineteenth
century. From roof of merry-go-round
in park at Greenfield, Massachusetts.
Length: thirty inches. (*Shelburne
Museum*)

Horse. Copper with traces of gilding.
Vane is attributed to L. Harris and
Sons, Boston. Length: twenty-nine inches.
(*Ross Levett*)

Horse, painted sheet iron. Nineteenth
century. Pointer represents turf.

Man on horseback vane was called "Civilian" by Fiske in 1893 catalog.

Saddle horse and lady rider. Three-quarter full-bodied gilded copper vane made by Fiske was available in any size.

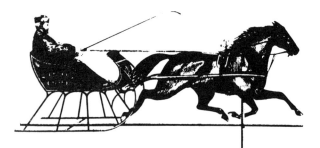

Trotter to sleigh, three-quarter full-bodied. Copper with gilding. From 1893 Fiske Company catalog. Length: forty-one inches.

Trotter to road wagon was another 1893 Fiske design. Length: forty-four inches.

"Horse over Hurdle" vane by Fiske was design later adapted by silhouette vane-designers. Gilded copper in thirty-inch length or any size to order. Fiske.

Running horse and jockey. Horse has banged tail. Length: thirty-one inches. Fiske catalog of 1893.

Horse vane, copper. Possibly famous trotter, "Dexter." Nineteenth century. Length: thirty inches. (*Harold Cole*)

Currier and Ives lithograph of the trotting horse "Dexter." Weather-vane makers frequently copied their models from these prints. Lithograph dated 1865.

Trotting horse, "Goldsmith's Maid," is copper and was made in late nineteenth century. Length: thirty-two inches.

Man on horseback made in last quarter of nineteenth century. Painted galvanized iron. Length: thirty-two and a half inches. (*Smithsonian Institution*)

Horse, copper, probably regilded. Late
nineteenth century. Length:
thirty-one inches.

Horse. Copper. Nineteenth century.
Scrollwork on cardinal points indicates
maker as W. A. Snow, of Boston. Note
bullet holes in hindquarter of horse.
(*Blackberry River Inn, Norfolk,
Connecticut*)

Horse and sulky. Copper. Nineteenth
century. Less detailed than Fiske vane.
Possibly made by E. G. Washburne.

Horse and sulky, copper. Made in
nineteenth century by J. W. Fiske
Company. Length: forty-two inches.
(*William R. Moody*)

Trotting horse, "Mountain Boy." Made by J. W. Fiske Company in last quarter of nineteenth century. Copper. Length: thirty-three inches. (*John A. Coe*)

Currier and Ives lithograph showing trotting horse with four-wheeled sulky. Probably used to make model of vane presently at Citizens Bank, Providence, Rhode Island.

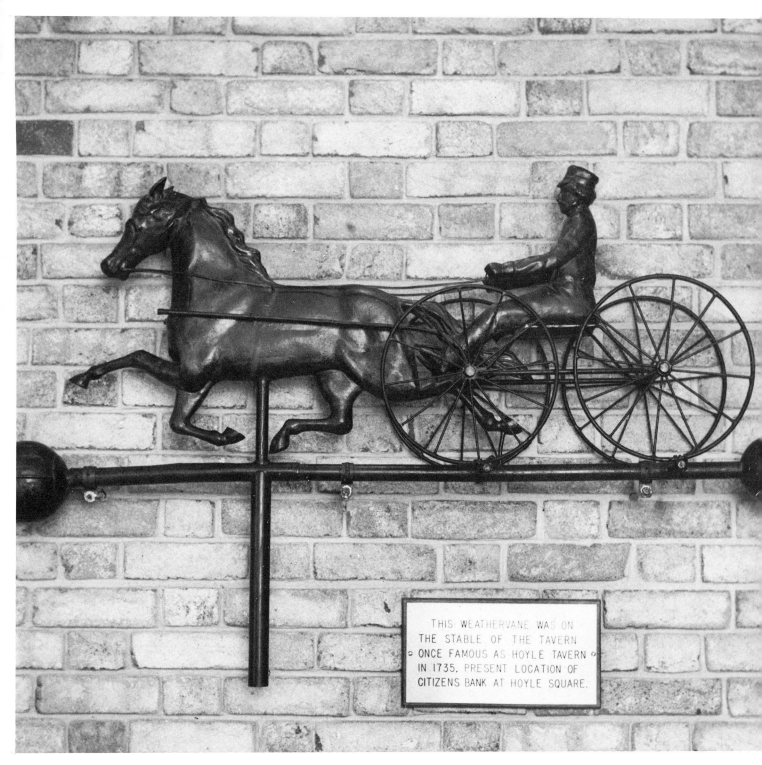

THIS WEATHERVANE WAS ON
THE STABLE OF THE TAVERN
ONCE FAMOUS AS HOYLE TAVERN
IN 1735. PRESENT LOCATION OF
CITIZENS BANK AT HOYLE SQUARE.

Horse with very rare four-wheeled
sulky. Nineteenth-century photographs
show vane on barn behind inn at Hoyle
Square, Providence, Rhode Island. Vane
is on display in lobby of Citizens
Bank, which was built on site
of former inn.

110

Model of "Nashua," famous racehorse,
mounted on clubhouse of Keeneland
Racing Association, Lexington, Kentucky.
Vane is five feet long and is made of
sheet copper. Built in 1971 by Kenneth
Lynch and Sons, Incorporated.

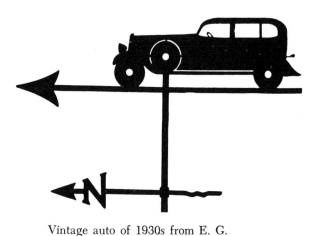

Vintage auto of 1930s from E. G. Washburne silhouette catalog. Vanes with later model cars are extremely rare, although catalog offered to make any model to order.

Horse car was advertised as vane in 1893 Fiske Company catalog. Described as "perfect model with pair of horses attached and driver and conductor." It could be made to order in any size.

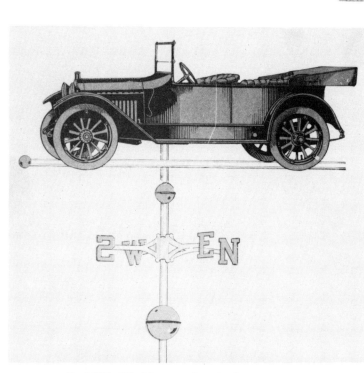

In 1920s Washburne advertised vanes such as this as "Automobile." Full-bodied gilded copper.

Rare weather vane is full-bodied copper model of 1909 Hupmobile. Length: forty-eight inches. (*Bihler and Conger*)

Page from E. G. Washburne catalog of 1920s showing two automobile weather vanes and prices. Few of these were made, and they are worth many times their original price today.

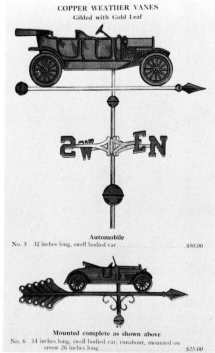

COPPER WEATHER VANES
Gilded with Gold Leaf

Automobile
No. 5 32 inches long, swell bodied car $50.00

Mounted complete as shown above
No. 6 14 inches long, swell bodied car, runabout, mounted on
arrow 26 inches long $25.00

112

Vane of old-time motorist is of modern manufacture. Litchfield Farm Shops, Connecticut.

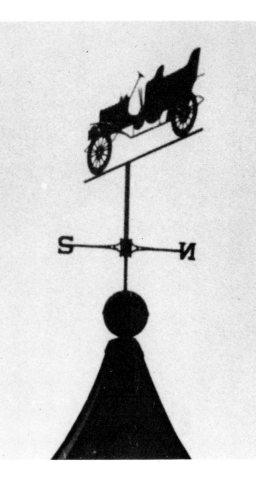

Early model automobile is located on building housing Buick dealer in East Hampton, Long Island, New York.

Duplicate of vane representing U-2 reconnaissance airplane. Original vane presented to Francis Gary Powers, pilot of U-2 shot down over U.S.S.R. in 1958. Made by Kenneth Lynch and Sons, Incorporated.

113

11

BARNYARD ANIMALS

In the late nineteenth century the American rural skyline might have resembled a gilded copper barnyard. During this period many weather vanes were made in the profiles of cows, hogs, and sheep. It is obvious that to the American farmer no figure was more noble than his favorite barnyard animal. These bulky and rather ungraceful animals, which were the farmer's livelihood, were given the honored place on the cupolas of the buildings that housed them.

By the middle of the nineteenth century a farm was no longer just a place where the owner grew food only for his own family and raised animals to provide milk and meat for his own table. Around the middle of the century cattle were imported to America in order to develop large herds that would provide food for the urban areas of a country with a rapidly growing population. The breeds of cattle that we think of as American were brought to this country from Switzerland, the Netherlands, and England. Farms became factories for the production of milk and its by-products, and great herds were bred for beef. Cattle ranching and breeding became big business, and huge barns were built to house the great herds necessary for the marketing of beef and milk products.

Weather-vane manufacturers were able to supply suitable vane motifs as decoration for the elaborate barns built after the middle of the nineteenth century. It is probable that, as with many other specialized weather vanes one finds in the early catalogs, many of the cow and bull vanes were made to order for a particular customer, and the vane was then advertised in the manufacturers' catalogs in the hope of selling more so that the cost of the molds could be amortized.

Most cow weather vanes were made after the middle of the nineteenth century. The majority were elaborately molded copper vanes made by the major manufacturers, or they were adapted by home craftsmen from the manufactured cow vanes. The Jersey, Guernsey, Holstein, Ayreshire, and Brown Swiss cattle of the successful breeders were sometimes commemmorated by special weather vanes made in the shapes characteristic of the breed. The Fiske catalog for 1893 shows a bull vane called "Bull" and two cow vanes called simply "Cow." However, there is another weather vane called "Short Horned Jersey Cow." It would have been difficult for the affluent farmer who specialized in this breed to resist decorating his barn with a vane that announced to passersby the breed of cattle that comprised his herd.

A successful hog farmer was no less enamored of the rather ungraceful animal from which he earned his livelihood, and more than one manufacturer of weather vanes advertised vanes called "Hog." Those breeders who earned their living by the meat products of these fecund Suidae saw beauty in their figures. These hog vanes were made as trade signs as well as building decorations. As is true of the cow vanes, those with sow or boar motifs are from the latter half of the nineteenth century and are three-quarter- or half-round-bodied copper that was originally gilded.

Sheep weather vanes were appropriate not only for the farmer who bred the animal but also for the factories that processed its wool and wove it into cloth. A large ram vane, which is on exhibit at the Shelburne Museum, was taken from the woolen mill in Livermore Falls, Maine. Molds were made for vanes that venerated prize rams that had become famous among the breeders of that animal in the United States.

In addition to the large and elaborate copper full-bodied weather vanes in the shapes of cows, hogs, and sheep, there are numerous small vanes with similar motifs that were designed and manufactured to ornament the lightning rods that prudent farmers attached to their barn roofs. Many of these small zinc animals were sold as complete units of cupola–vane–lightning rod. The cupolas were really prefabricated ventilators that were an essential part of barn construction. These vane–rod–ventilator combinations could be purchased through mail order catalogs from Montgomery Ward or Sears Roebuck. Interesting examples of these small animal vanes still abound on barns in areas of the Northeast. Some were made with the added decoration of blown glass balls in clear, amber, red, and green.

The miniature zinc animals were made from molds that were similar to the larger farm animal figures for weather vanes and were produced by the same companies. One manufacturer of these small animal figures reminisced recently that he made quantities of these animals at the beginning of this century and sold them to the lightning-rod manufacturer for eighteen cents apiece. The manufacturer in turn sold the animals for fifty-four cents. "It would be impossible today," the original manufacturer lamented, "to reproduce one of these animals for fifty-four dollars."

To the farmer who purchased these lightning rods and ventilators, the small sheep, cow, or hog vane that decorated them was an added bonus. It is a tribute to the men who produced these small figures that so many of them are still standing. It is probable that as collectors begin to realize that even these relatively inexpensive animal weather-vane decorations have an important place in the business and agricultural history of our country, the little zinc cows, sheep, and hogs will be brought down off the rooftops of dilapidated barns to be placed in collections with their larger, more elaborate counterparts.

Copper cow weather vane was victim of gunshot. Found in Colchester, Vermont. Tail and horns are brass. Length: twenty-four inches; height: twelve inches. (*Shelburne Museum*)

Cow vane, made in last half of nineteenth century. Gilded copper. Length: thirty-six inches.

Cow on arrow. Iron and gilded
copper vane and lightning rod. "James"
identifies maker.

Gilded copper cow vane and lightning
rod is part of elaborate metal ventilator.

"Hog" vane was advertised by Fiske in 1893 catalog. It was made in three-quarter full-bodied copper and was gilded. It was made in two sizes: thirty-four inches and forty inches in length.

Cow from Fiske catalog of 1893. Copper, gilded, made in full-bodied or one-half or three-quarter bodied.

"Boar" vane by Fiske. Three-quarter full-bodied gilded copper. Length: thirty inches.

COPPER WEATHER VANES

Gilded with Gold Leaf

Hog

In 1920 E. G. Washburne advertised this hog vane at prices from thirty-eight dollars to seventy-five dollars.

Prize Merino ram was subject for Fiske weather vane in 1893. Length: thirty inches.

No. 150	30 inches long	$38.00
No. 151	36 inches long	45.00
No. 152	42 inches long	62.00
No. 153	48 inches long	75.00

Hog vane in painted sheet iron
made by amateur craftsman. Latter half
of nineteenth century. Length:
thirty-two and a half inches.
(*Smithsonian Institution*)

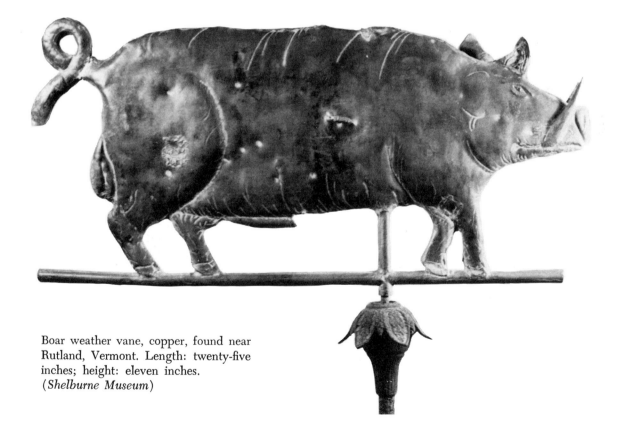

Boar weather vane, copper, found near
Rutland, Vermont. Length: twenty-five
inches; height: eleven inches.
(*Shelburne Museum*)

Merino ram made by manufacturer in latter half of nineteenth century. Gilded copper. Length: twenty-nine inches.

Merino ram from Addison County, Vermont. Body is sheet copper, and head is cast zinc. Length: twenty-seven inches. (*Shelburne Museum*)

Ram, gilded copper, from woolen mills in Livermore Falls, Maine. Legs are painted black. One-quarter round copper. (*Shelburne Museum*)

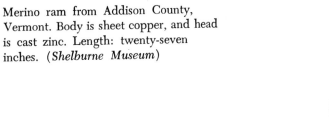

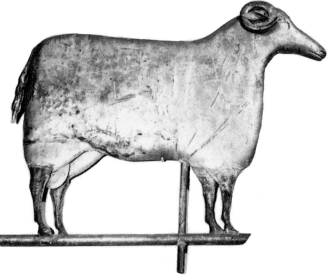

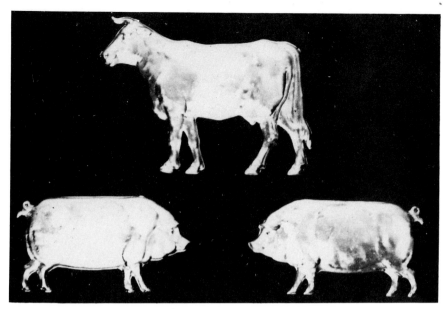

Small molded animals made by
Kenneth Lynch and Sons, Incorporated,
to decorate vanes on lightning rods
made for barns around 1920

Plow weather vane was made in
latter half of nineteenth century. Length:
fifty-five and three-quarter inches.
(*Smithsonian Institution*)

Combination lightning rod and weather
vane was made by the Indiana Bins
Division of the Martin–Marietta
Company, and many farms carry this
free advertising on their silos.

12

FISH VANES

Fish weather vanes abound on buildings along the Atlantic seacoast. Since the economy of many of the coast towns and cities depends upon the products of the sea, the fish is an obvious subject for weather vanes in this area. Moreover, the fish shape is ideal as a weather-vane configuration that can easily be balanced and has a head and tail that can point wind direction as clearly as an arrow.

Perhaps the most famous of all primitive fish weather vanes is the wooden fish that once was studded with copper nails and stood above Paul Revere's shop. Many equally primitive wooden fish vanes still stand on the buildings on which they were originally placed. The simple fish shape seems to withstand weathering better than more elaborate motifs.

One primitive fish vane on a barn in the inland town of Watertown, Connecticut, dates from the eighteenth century and is in remarkable condition for its age. It has been painted over and over and has a few minor repairs, but its simple profile shape is still as it originally was carved by an amateur craftsman over two hundred years ago. It might be noted here that although fish motif vanes abound along the waterfront, the fish has long been considered a good luck symbol, and there are hundreds of fish vanes on buildings that are far removed from either ocean.

Stylized silhouettes of flounder, cod, and swordfish as well as other fish have been the subject of weather vanes for many years. Most of the fish used as vane subjects are those that have sleek lines that adapt easily as vane motifs. Certain kinds of fish that are found in quantity in a particular area will be found in abundance on vanes in that area.

Another carved wood weather vane of a fish in the Shelburne Museum collection came from a Maine coast island and was made in the eighteenth century. An interesting nineteenth-century hand-crafted fish in full round from the same collection was fashioned from sheets of tin that were painted gray. A copper codfish with traces of gilt was made around the middle of the nineteenth century and came, not surprisingly, from Boston.

Just as the smaller fish that earned the livelihood for many inhabitants of seacoasts were immortalized as weather-vane motifs, so the towns along the coast that sent ships out in search of the great whales in the eighteenth and nineteenth centuries made weather monuments to that sea animal. The towns along the Atlantic seacoast that were great centers for the whaling industry still display on their rooftops examples of whale weather vanes. Long Island, New York, whaling towns such as Sag Harbor were totally dependent upon the whale as a means of support, and perhaps one of the first sights the incoming whalers might see would be the silhouette of the great whale rising above his town in the form of a weather vane.

Both the right whale and the sperm whale were carved or molded into weather-vane subjects and were used on houses and barns as well as municipal buildings and churches. One interesting weather vane with a whale motif decorates a shingled windmill in Bridgehampton, Long Island. In the whaling towns during the eighteenth and nineteenth centuries the entire population was reliant upon the luck of the whalers who were forced to go farther and farther in search of a catch, and the vanes were erected as a mark of respect, not only for the men who went to sea, but for the great sea mammal that they sought.

In the latter half of the nineteenth century the major manufacturers of weather vanes did not neglect the fish as a popular subject for their gilded copper full-bodied vanes, and a great many fish vanes still exist from that period. Since the manufacturers were selling weather vanes and not fish, they evidently did not feel obliged to advertise their vanes by any more explicit name than "Fish." It is interesting to compare the early catalog engravings with the real weather vanes from that period. One can see the liberties the mold-makers took when adapting an artist's rendering to the medium in which they had to work. The Fiske catalog fish vane illustrated here along with its manufactured counterpart has larger, more stylized scales, and the tail fin has been somewhat simplified. While the catalog artist was interested in a faithful, realistic rendering of the subject, the craftsman was more concerned with presenting a finished product that when viewed from some distance would give the same general appearance as the artist's drawing. Moreover, there were certain technical problems involved in hammering copper into a mold with which the original designer did not seem to concern himself.

The swordfish and the dolphin are two fish that have been used as weather-vane motifs, but they are not as common as other types of fish vanes. The swordfish is something of a latecomer as a weather-vane motif, but the handsome dolphin illustrated here is late nineteenth century and came from Yarmouthport, Massachusetts. It is made of molded copper sheets, and the parts were soldered to form the full-bodied shape. This vane has been reproduced in aluminum by the Lynch firm.

One can see from modern weather vanes that have been made by individual craftsmen that the fish form is as appealing to today's vane-makers as it was to those of the eighteenth century. The great sculptor Alexander Calder adapted the traditional fish form when making the metal weather vane illustrated in this chapter for one of his Connecticut neighbors. The Calder fish is highly stylized in silhouette form with pierced work and is a rather amusing product of a sculptor who now works with massive abstract shapes and forms in metal.

This wooden fish vane was once on the roof of Paul Revere's workshop. It was originally studded with copper nails to resemble scales. It is now on display in the Revere home in Boston, Massachusetts.

Fish vane, made of painted wood, is late eighteenth century and is in use in inland town of Watertown, Connecticut. (*Hayden Alexander*)

Early nineteenth-century weather vane has good luck symbols of fish and hand of God. (*Scudder Smith*)

Codfish vane, full-bodied. Tin, painted gray. Nineteenth century. Length: thirty-three inches. (*Shelburne Museum*)

Gilded copper codfish, made around 1850, was found in Boston. (*Shelburne Museum*)

125

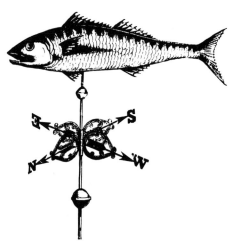

Fish weather vane advertised by
Fiske in 1893

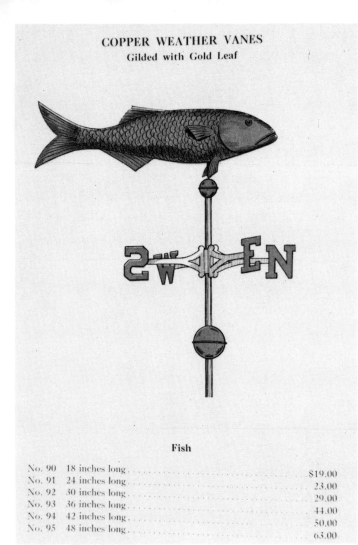

COPPER WEATHER VANES
Gilded with Gold Leaf

Fish

No. 90	18 inches long	$19.00
No. 91	24 inches long	23.00
No. 92	30 inches long	29.00
No. 93	36 inches long	44.00
No. 94	42 inches long	50.00
No. 95	48 inches long	63.00

Fish weather vane from 1920s
Washburne catalog

Silhouette of fish is vane from the
1920s. Highly stylized form. Kenneth
Lynch and Sons, Incorporated.

Swordfish silhouette vane. This is from
Washburne's 1930 catalog, but several
makers made similar vanes at the time.

Spouting whale vane called "Cape Cod"
by its maker, Kenneth Lynch, is
reproduction of antique made in
sheet iron.

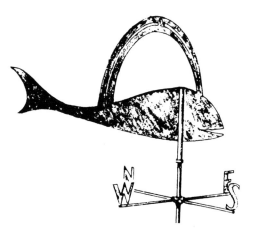

126

Carved wood fish weather vane. Made
by Read Manufacturing Company in
nineteenth century. Full round body
thirteen and a half inches long.
(*Shelburne Museum*)

Fish vane made by Fiske shows
liberties vane-maker took with artist's
rendition. (*Shelburne Museum*)

Whale vane made from four pieces of
tin. Found in Old Lyme, Connecticut.
Made in first half of nineteenth century.
Length: twenty-three inches.
(*Shelburne Museum*)

Shingled windmill in Bridgehampton,
Long Island, has whale vane as symbol
of early local industry. Close-up view, (below)
shows whale to be made of one piece
of wood.

128

Whale vane from New England.
Copper applied over wood. Nineteenth
century. (*Allan L. Daniel*)

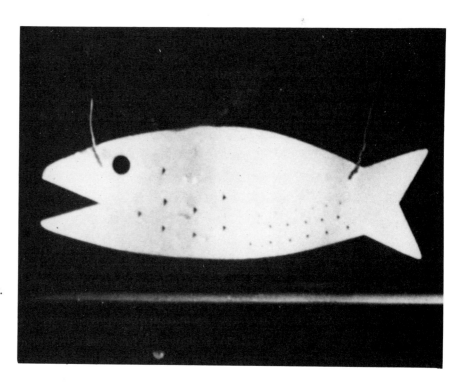

Amusing metal fish vane was made
by sculptor Alexander Calder for
a neighbor in Woodbury, Connecticut.

Rare weather vane made of tin is in form of shark. (*Shelburne Museum*)

Dolphin vane, copper, is from Yarmouthport, Massachusetts. It is made of two sheets of copper soldered together. This unusual vane has been reproduced by Kenneth Lynch and Sons, Incorporated. (*Shelburne Museum*)

Carved wooden fish vane, made in first quarter of this century in Vermont, has copper fins and scales. (*John Kannengeiser*)

Sophisticated seagull ignores swordfish
vane on Howard's Fish Market in
East Hampton, Long Island.

13

UNUSUAL BIRDS
AND OTHER ANIMALS

Besides the rooster, the eagle, and the goose, there is one other bird that figures rather strongly as a weather-vane subject. Because he has a connotation that differs from his other more popular feathered relatives, the owl should be considered separately as a subject for weather-vane motifs. The eagle symbolizes strength and is a national symbol, while the rooster vanes had their origins in religion. The owl has become associated in legend with wisdom and intelligence. This probably has more to do with the bird's wide-eyed appearance than any special characteristics he displays, since the owl doesn't seem to be any more intelligent than other birds.

Owl vanes are mostly of late nineteenth-century vintage, and many vanes with owl motifs were made somewhat later. As a weather-vane motif the owl has been produced from time to time to decorate libraries and schools. A prominent owl vane sits atop the Sterling Library of Yale University in New Haven, Connecticut, to announce that wise people dwell within and perhaps to give credence to the saying that "all wisdom is contained in books." The Yale owl's perch is an elaborately designed wrought iron arrow above even more elaborate cardinal points. In contrast to the dark iron, the copper owl gives one the impression that he is only resting on the arrow temporarily and might fly off any minute. In reality he is permanently anchored to the massive arrow vane.

Other owl weather vanes have been made by individual craftsmen as well as by the silhouette vane manufacturers who worked during the first part of this century. A superb hand-crafted weather vane of a family of three owls in silhouette decorates the Postcard

Museum in Canaan, Connecticut. The building was constructed during the late nineteenth century, and the vane was probably installed when the building was originally erected.

Another arrow silhouette vane comprising a larger family of five owls can be seen on a private dwelling in Goshen, Connecticut, and is a manufacturer's product dating around 1920. Several manufacturers made this type of vane, although usually with fewer owls on each vane. The perch is a naturalistic iron standard made to look like a tree branch. The vane with two owls in silhouette illustrated here is a superb example of the stylized silhouette vanes that are typical of the period preceding the Second World War. Some of the weather-vane manufacturers still in business make new vanes with owls as the motifs, and several of them still use the early patterns.

If the owls connoted wisdom, weather vanes with peacock motifs represent the less desirable qualities of vanity and pride. Although the peacock was a motif generally used around the turn of the century and is usually thought of as an art nouveau motif, an interesting peacock weather vane that dates from around 1800 is owned by the Shelburne Museum. This is a Connecticut vane and is handmade of lead and copper with feather designs chiseled into the copper tail. A peacock weather vane from any period is rare, and although there is one advertised in the 1893 Fiske Company catalog, it is doubtful that many of these vanes were made.

Other birds that made their way to the tops of a few buildings are pigeons, swans, and ostriches. These were all late nineteenth-century motifs that gave the new home-builder a welcome relief from the more ubiquitous eagle and rooster. George Washington chose a dove in flight with an olive branch in its mouth for the weather vane that was installed on top of his house at Mount Vernon.

The late nineteenth century was also a period when there was a great interest in exotic and unusual animals from other lands. Weather vanes were offered to its clientele by the Fiske Company with motifs of elephants and lions. In order to capture the western market, bears and buffalo were also available in realistic full-round copper sculptures.

Except for the grasshopper weather vane made by Shem Drowne which has already been discussed and the many manufacturers' versions of the famous Boston weather vane, there have been few other vanes made in the shapes of insects. One exception is the butterfly weather vane that can be seen at the Shelburne Museum. This vane was originally from New Hampshire and is made of copper that is pierced and striated. From a study of a drawing of a similar vane in the Fiske Company catalog of 1893 one can assume that the

Shelburne vane was manufactured by that company in the late nineteenth century. Although the piercing in the actual vane is not identical with that of the drawing in the catalog, one must keep in mind that the vanes in the early catalogs were only artist's renderings of vane designs and that there were always variations in the actual making of the vanes themselves.

Oddly enough, cats were not common subjects for nineteenth-century weather vanes, perhaps because of the superstitions connected with them. The magnificent vane illustrated here of a member of the cat family is rare and unusual. Although it is undoubtedly a nineteenth-century manufacturer's vane, it has yet to be seen in any of the early catalogs and might have been a special order.

All of the less common bird and animal weather vanes that we find illustrated in the early catalogs, in museum and private collections, and those we still see on rooftops that date from the nineteenth century comprise a minute percentage of the animal vanes that were produced in that prolific period. Most purchasers of weather vanes of the period stuck to weather vanes with more conventional motifs.

Handmade iron owl weather vane on roof of Postcard Museum in Canaan, Connecticut.

Elaborate Monel Metal and iron vane with owl sits atop Sterling Library at Yale University, New Haven, Connecticut. Made about 1930 by Samuel Yellin, one of America's greatest ironworkers.

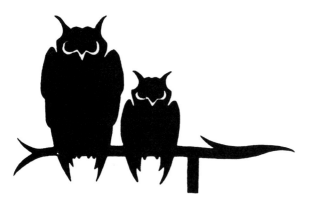

Superb silhouette owls form vane made by Kenneth Lynch and Sons, Incorporated. Length: twenty-seven inches. Made around 1930.

Owl on broom comprised vane that was advertised in 1893 Fiske Company catalog. Length: three feet. Full-bodied gilded copper.

Mother owl and two babies sit on branch-shaped vane on house in Pikesville, Maryland.

Family of five owls on weather vane in Goshen, Connecticut

This silhouette vane of a swan on water is of the period around 1920–1930. Made by Kenneth Lynch and Sons, Incorporated.

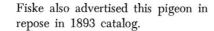

Fiske also advertised this pigeon in repose in 1893 catalog.

Peacock vane was made by Fiske in late nineteenth century in any size the customer wanted. Gilded copper.

Peacock weather vane was found in Connecticut and dates from around 1800. The body is lead, and the tail is copper, one-sixteenth of an inch thick. (*Shelburne Museum*)

George Washington chose a dove with an olive branch, the international symbol of peace, as motif for vane at Mount Vernon.

Goose weather vane. Midwest,
nineteenth century. Made of two sheets
of tin riveted to iron support.
(*Cincinnati Art Museum, Carol C.
Guggenheim Memorial Fund*)

Design for butterfly vane was in 1893 Fiske Company catalog.

This ostrich weather vane was available from Fiske in 1893. It is doubtful, however, that many were made. Length: three feet six inches.

Elephant vane in full-bodied gilded copper was offered to Fiske Company's customers in 1893. It came in two sizes: twenty-eight inches and thirty-four inches long.

By the 1930s the Lynch firm was making this playful silhouette elephant vane.

Lion weather vane from Fiske Company was made in three- or four-foot size.

Rabbit silhouette is sleek Art Deco design of 1920s. Made by Kenneth Lynch.

Silhouette of goat seems to be only vane made of that animal. Made by Kenneth Lynch and Sons, Incorporated.

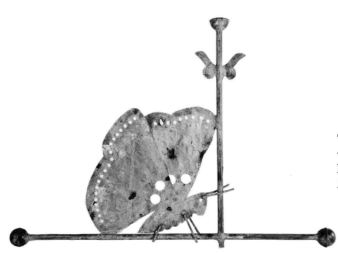

This pierced copper butterfly weather vane was probably made by Fiske in late nineteenth century. (*Shelburne Museum*)

The cat seemed to be neglected as a weather-vane subject. This rare vane was made around 1890. (*Bihler and Conger*)

14

HUNTERS AND THE HUNTED

It should come as no surprise that the American Indian was a popular subject for some of the earliest handmade weather vanes that we have. The early settlers in America were indebted to the Indian for their very existence. It was from the Indian that the settlers learned to hunt and fish. Methods of growing and storing food for the long and difficult New England winters were also learned by observing the Indian.

Long before commercial weather vanes were made, the Indian was a frequent subject for primitive weather vanes. The earliest Indian vane that can be attributed to its maker is the previously mentioned Shem Drowne Indian that once adorned the rooftop of the Province House in Boston. However, it is probable that a few of the handmade weather vanes that still exist with Indians as subjects were made previous to Shem Drowne's time.

Indians as subjects for weather vanes are most often shown as hunters with bow and arrow poised for the kill. The early settlers in this country were as dependent upon game for meat as were the Indians, and the Indian's prowess in procuring game was undoubtedly highly admired by the first generations of white American settlers.

There is another reason that we find so many primitive Indian vanes: The figure of an Indian poised with bow and arrow was eminently suitable as a two-dimensional functional vane. The body of the Indian provides a good windbreak, and proper balance could be achieved by designing the headdress on one side and the bow and arrow on the other to give the same approximate weight to both sides of the figure. In addition, the arrow provides a directional signal that is helpful in determining the wind direction.

The profile shapes used in the two-dimensional Indian figures made it easy to distinguish just what the figure is supposed to represent without requiring too much detail. A few jagged edges around the top of the head indicate a feather headdress. In some of the early vanes the arrow becomes an extension of the Indian's arm. The figure of the Indian can be found in either a standing, kneeling, or running position in primitive weather vanes that exist today.

When factory-made weather vanes came on the scene in the middle of the nineteenth century, few were made with Indians as subjects. The one that is most often seen is the full-bodied copper Indian with a bow in one hand and a large arrow in the other. He is shown not as an active hunter but as a national symbol. An excellent example of this vane can be seen at the Shelburne Museum in Vermont. Very few examples of this weather vane exist today, and the Shelburne Indian vane is especially important since portions of the same vane have been shown recently as an example of a "complete" vane in the *Index of American Design.* However, the *Index* drawing is missing many parts, including his bow, his arrow, and a grouping of a log and vegetation that once stood next to him. The completed weather vane makes a superbly balanced composition.

Toward the end of the nineteenth century the commercial weather-vane makers had all but forgotten the debt the white man owed the Indian, and hunters as sportsmen were, instead, immortalized on these later weather vanes. The gun replaces the Indian's arrow as a directional signal. The Smithsonian Institution has an example of a white hunter-sportsman that was made by hand in the late nineteenth century. By the time this vane was made, Americans no longer had to hunt in order to obtain meat, but hunting as a sport had become popular.

In addition to the hunter, his dogs and his prey were subjects of weather vanes made after 1850. A gilded iron weather vane of a full-bodied hunting dog is in the Smithsonian Institution collection and illustrates the veneration hunters have always had for their dogs. A pointing dog also made a good subject for a weather vane that was directional and well-balanced. Figure vanes of dogs chasing foxes or deer were also popular in the late nineteenth century and were made by more than one weather-vane company.

The early twentieth-century silhouette vane-designers were able to tell more complete hunting stories. A hunter and his dog can be found stalking their prey on one silhouette vane. Another hunting scene, designed and made by the Garrett Thew Studios, shows a hunter and his dog waiting patiently for their decoys to draw some game.

The hunted as well as the hunter were subjects for weather vanes. There are many primitive examples of deer weather vanes. On some of these early vanes the stag is standing still while in later manufactured vanes the modeler was able to depict the stag as a graceful, leaping subject. Groups of geese also made graceful weather-vane subjects, and this theme has been used frequently throughout the history of weather-vane design.

Shem Drowne's famous Indian, made
in 1716 for Province House in Boston.
Four feet six inches high. (*Massachusetts
Historical Society, Boston*)

Indian with bow and raised tomahawk
made in latter half of nineteenth
century. Painted tin and plated steel.
Height: forty-eight and three-eighth
inches. (*Shelburne Museum*)

Early nineteenth-century "Tote" weather vane. "Improved Order of Redmen." Length: thirty-one inches; height: fifty-one inches. Painted sheet iron. (*Shelburne Museum*)

Indian archer made around 1810. Height: sixty inches. Sheet iron with copper bow. Riveted and painted. (*Shelburne Museum*)

Indian weather vane made around 1840. Amateur carved of one piece of wood with moving arms for balance. Height: thirty-nine inches. (*Shelburne Museum*)

143

Indian with drawn bow. Made during latter half of nineteenth century. Painted iron. Height: eighteen inches. (*Smithsonian Institution*)

Indian with drawn bow. Made during latter half of nineteenth century. (*Ryther House Antiques*)

144

Handmade Indian vane. Wood.
First half of nineteenth century.

Hunter with bow, possibly meant to be
Robin Hood, is made of painted iron.

145

Chief Tammany. Figure is nine feet tall. Made before Civil War. Once stood on political clubhouse in East Branch, New York. (*Museum of American Folk Art*)

Massasoit, made by Harris in Boston, Massachusetts, in late nineteenth century. Copper. Taken from Uncas Hotel, Norwich, Connecticut. (*Shelburne Museum*)

Reproduction of Indian "Tote" vane is used on building at Shelburne Museum.

Sheet-iron silhouette of hunter in
coonskin cap. Length: fifty-four inches.
Late nineteenth century.

Hunter vane is painted iron silhouette.
Made in last quarter of the nineteenth
century. Height: twenty-six and
three-eighth inches. (*Smithsonian
Institution*)

Silhouette vane of hunter and his dog is painted copper or aluminum. On building in Bethlehem, Connecticut.

Silhouette of hunter and his dog was made by Garrett Thew Studios in Connecticut around 1930.

Hound chasing fox. Gilded copper.
Latter half of nineteenth century.
(*Harold Cole*)

Gilded copper hollow-bodied hunting
dog vane was made in latter half of
nineteenth century. (*Allan L. Daniel*)

Hound and fox vane on Rice Lumber
Yard in Shelburne, Vermont. Probably
made by L. W. Cushing Company.

Hunting dog vane made around 1940 is
iron, painted black and white.

150

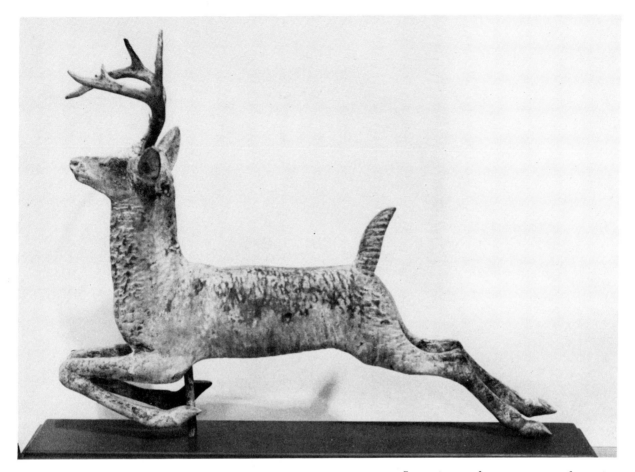

Late nineteenth-century vane of running deer probably made by Fiske Company. (*Ryther House Antiques*)

Deer weather vane made in mid-nineteenth century. Sheet iron with wrought iron bands for support. Twenty-nine and three-quarters inches high. (*Shelburne Museum*)

151

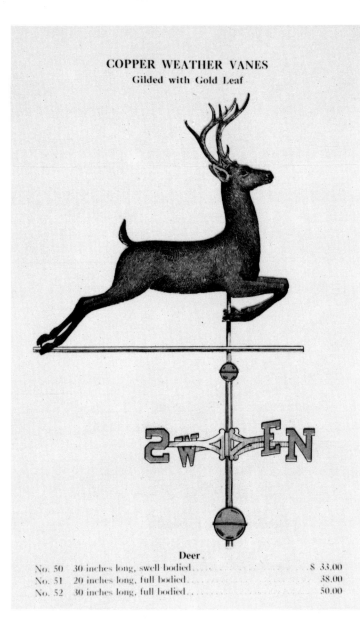

COPPER WEATHER VANES
Gilded with Gold Leaf

Deer

No. 50	30 inches long, swell-bodied	$ 33.00
No. 51	20 inches long, full bodied	38.00
No. 52	30 inches long, full bodied	50.00

Full-bodied deer vane made by
Washburne in 1920

Running deer vane made of copper,
possibly by Washburne.

Deer silhouette. Painted sheet iron.
Maine, late nineteenth century.

In 1893 Fiske Company offered one Indian vane in catalog. Made in three-quarter, full-bodied copper, the vane was three feet six inches high, and arrow was five feet six inches long.

Deer and hound vane. Fiske, 1893.

Fiske's buffalo vane was made in three-quarter full bodied. Thirty-four inches in length.

Bear vane by Fiske from 1893 catalog. Length: twenty-eight inches.

Flying goose. Made in nineteenth
century of wood with tin tail. Length:
eighty-four inches. (*Shelburne Museum*)

Handsome twentieth-century vane was
designed and made by noted bird artist
Rex Brasher. Painted, carved wood.
(*Tanner House, Warren, Connecticut*)

Pheasant weather vane (or possibly
rooster) is early nineteenth century and
made of sheet iron. Length: twenty-nine
inches. (*Smithsonian Institution*)

15

MYTHOLOGICAL AND RELIGIOUS FIGURES

Of all the subjects used for weather vanes perhaps the most unusual and charming are those of angels, gods and goddesses, and other characters from mythology. This group, particularly in the primitive weather vanes, allowed the makers free rein on their imagination. Without access to art reference books or pictures of the images they wished to create, wood-carvers and metal-workers made highly individualistic versions of these forms.

One of the earliest and most frequently produced ecclesiastical subjects was the angel Gabriel. In the horizontal aspect in which he is generally seen he is gracefully carried by his wings over the building he adorns with his trumpet pointing into the wind. Among the earliest-known Gabriel vanes is an amusing flat wood cut-out figure in the Shelburne Museum collection. Dating from about 1800, the figure is a caricature with a disproportionately large head and a considerably shortened body. Found in Ridgefield, Connecticut, it still bears traces of the original bold painting around the eyes, ears, and hem of its gown.

The most famous and controversial Gabriel vane is presently located on the People's Methodist Church in Newburyport, Massachusetts. It was originally built for the Universalist Church in that town in 1840 by the Boston firm of Gould and Hazlett. It is six feet and two inches long, weighs thirty-eight pounds, and was made of a flat sheet of gilded copper a little more than one-sixteenth of an inch thick. The trumpet, however, was made in the full round.

After a number of years the church building was abandoned and the vane was put in storage in a local barn. Late in the nineteenth century a member of the People's Methodist Church saw the vane and managed to raise funds to buy it and install it on his church. There it stayed until 1937, when it was taken down to be painted as an example of American folk art for the *Index of American Design*. A Works Progress Administration Federal Arts Project artist, Lucille Chabot, made a watercolor painting of the now weathered greenish copper and gold vane that became one of the seventeen thousand renderings that make up the remarkable *Index* collection at the National Gallery of Art in Washington, D.C.

In 1965 the Post Office Department chose the *Index* painting of this weather vane for its Christmas stamp and printed 1,200,000,000 three-color copies. After the stamps were issued, someone called attention to the fact that the male angel Gabriel had female breasts. The Post Office Department checked the actual vane against the *Index* drawing and found that the artist had indeed rendered it accurately. This paradox was cause for humorous observations in several newspapers and was finally settled by opinions from experts that angels are spiritual, not corporeal, and likenesses of angels were a matter of artistic concern and not theological.

The L. W. Cushing version of the angel Gabriel is a particularly beautiful example. Done in copper in the half-round, it depicts Gabriel as a winged, naked cherub blowing his trumpet. The Smithsonian Institution dates its copy as being made in 1883 and reproduced its photograph for a Christmas card that it recently issued.

For other fanciful weather-vane subjects the early artists referred to figures from Greek and Roman mythology with a few astrological symbols also employed, The Smithsonian has a marvelously sleek, stylized gilded wood Pegasus, the Greek winged horse of the Muses. The painted sheet-iron version at the Shelburne Museum, while considerably cruder, is a vigorous rendition and a more practical weather vane. Shelburne also has outstanding examples of the zodiacal signs of Sagittarius and Pisces. The Sagittarius is a thirty-seven-inch-long rounded sheet-copper figure of a centaur ready to discharge an arrow from his bow. The Pisces is dated from the late eighteenth century and is painted sheet iron done in a quite sophisticated style.

The Shelburne Museum collection includes also an unusual eighteenth-century figure of the Greek sea god Triton. Originally from Newburyport, Massachusetts, it is interesting in three respects. First, it is made of pewter and is one of the very few vanes known to have been made from that alloy of tin and lead. Second, the half-man, half-fish figure is shown blowing a trumpet instead of the traditional conch shell. Finally, it is the same subject as that used in the earliest recorded weather vane, that of the Tower of the Winds in ancient Athens.

A modern rendition of the Roman sea god Neptune was formerly in the catalog of the Kenneth Lynch Company. This is a scaled-down silhouette version of the elaborate vane that Lynch made for a Newport, Rhode Island, mansion. Neptune's sea shell chariot is being pulled over the waves by an animal with the head and forelegs of a horse and the tail of a fish. This creature is remarkably similar to an old wooden vane of a sea serpent at Shelburne.

Another lovely creature of the sea is Shelburne's mermaid vane. It is fifty-two inches long, carved from a pine board one and seven-eighths inches thick, and is attributed to a mid-nineteenth-century wood-carver from Wayland, Massachusetts, named Warren Gould Rody. The figure has long streaming hair and is seen holding a comb in her right hand and a looking glass in the left. The surface of the mirror in which the mermaid is studying herself was originally polished copper.

The current Kenneth Lynch and Sons catalog offers a forty-inch painted aluminum copy of this weather vane that is remarkable in its fidelity to the wooden original. How Mr. Lynch was able to secure a mold of this vane, which is accurate down to every last crack and fissure of the larger original, makes a fascinating tale.

About fifteen years ago a Vermont architect became so enamored of this mermaid at Shelburne that he set about to carve an exact three-quarter-size duplicate. He spent three years on this project during which he made numerous trips to the museum to check his work. When the mermaid was completed, he brought it to the Lynch factory to have a metal copy made for his own house. Mr. Lynch agreed to do the job if he were permitted to cast a mold of the vane for his exclusive use. This was done, and anyone willing to spend $400 can have a reproduction of this exceptionally beautiful weather vane.

Nineteenth-century commercial vane-makers produced a limited variety of vanes with religious or mythological themes. The most numerous, of course, was the angel Gabriel. A few vanes were made of the winged Mercury and exotic beasts such as fire-breathing dragons and sea serpents. These vanes are rarely found today.

Reproduction of 1965 U.S. postage stamp representing angel Gabriel vane from People's Methodist Church in Newburyport, Massachusetts. Stamp caused controversy when issued because Gabriel has female shape. Original vane is copper, gilded. Length: six feet two inches. (*Dudley Atwood*)

Angel Gabriel, wood, circa 1800. Traces of original paint can be seen around eyes and hem of gown. Length: thirty-three and a half inches. (*Shelburne Museum*)

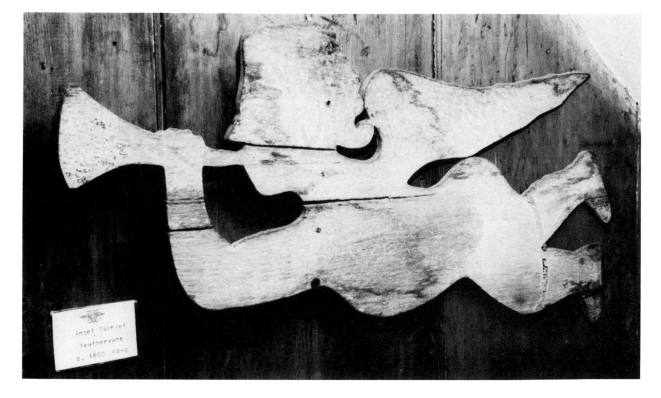

159

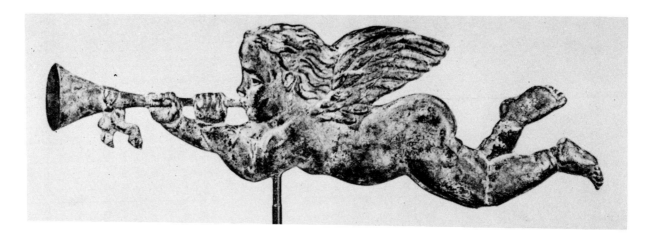

Angel Gabriel, made circa 1883 by
L. W. Cushing and Sons of Waltham,
Massachusetts. Hollow-body copper
vane was originally gilded. Length:
thirty-two inches. (*Smithsonian
Institution*)

Drawing of angel Gabriel atop the
Mormon Temple in Nauvoo, Illinois.
Engraving is dated 1848.

Angel Gabriel, late nineteenth century. Cast iron. Length: eighteen and a half inches. (*Smithsonian Institution*)

Wood angel Gabriel vane suggesting female form. (*Ryther House Antiques*)

Lion-killer, sheet iron, made in nineteenth century. Taken from Hampton, New Hampshire. Figure on horseback is supposed to represent Indian, but theme seems to be American version of St. George slaying the dragon. Length: thirty-eight and three-quarter inches. (*Shelburne Museum*)

This strange sheet-iron bird in the Shelburne Museum is called an eagle. Students of mythology have thought it to be a phoenix. Early nineteenth century. Length: twenty-four and a half inches.

Pegasus, nineteenth century, is gilded wood. Length: thirty-one and one-half inches. (*Smithsonian Institution*)

Wrought iron vane representing bishop's
mitre on Yale's Berkeley College.
College is named for Bishop Berkeley.

163

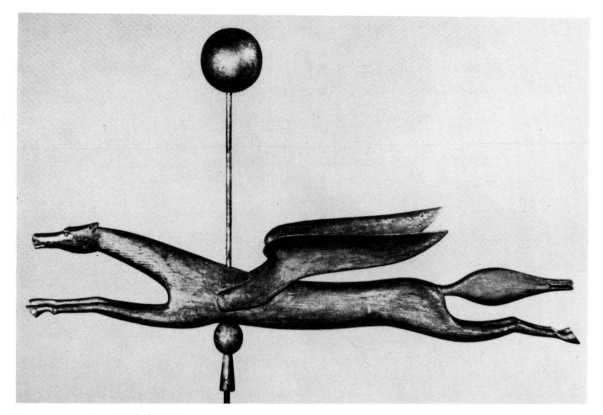

Pegasus vane is painted sheet iron
made in nineteenth century. Length:
thirty-five inches. (*Shelburne Museum*)

Centaur or zodiacal Sagittarius.
Hammered copper. Nineteenth century.
Length: thirty-seven inches. (*Shelburne Museum*)

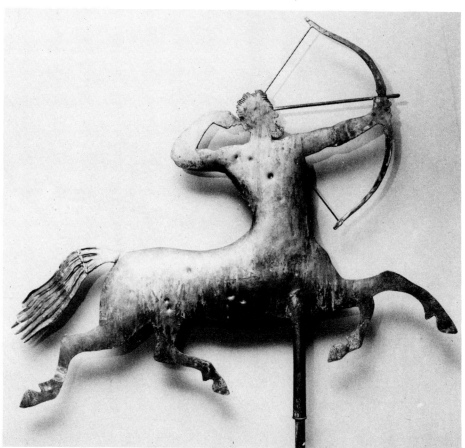

164

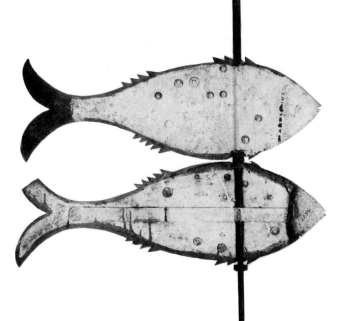

Zodiacal sign of Pisces. Sheet iron, made in late eighteenth century. Originally found in New York State. Length: thirty-three inches. (*Shelburne Museum*)

Sea serpent vane made of wood. Nineteenth century. Found in Milford, New Hampshire. Length: twenty-three and a half inches. (*Shelburne Museum*)

Triton, pewter. Mid-eighteenth-century vane from Newburyport, Massachusetts. Length: eighteen and a half inches. (*Shelburne Museum*)

Mermaid made in mid-nineteenth century. Attributed to Warren Gould Rody, of Wayland, Massachusetts. Carved pine, one and seven-eighths inches thick. Length: fifty-two and a half inches. (*Shelburne Museum*)

165

Figure of Mercury from 1893 Fiske catalog

Scaled down twenty-six-and-a-half-inch silhouette version of monumental eight-foot vane designed for Newport, Rhode Island, mansion. Designed by sculptor Pierre Bourdel and built by Kenneth Lynch and Sons, Incorporated.

Painted aluminum casting of line for line copy of original wood mermaid in Shelburne Museum. Made by Kenneth Lynch and Sons from wood carving done by Vermont architect. Length: forty inches.

Dragon weather vane was offered by Fiske Company to customers in three-feet-six-inch length in 1893.

166

16

SHIPS AND BOATS

A full-rigged sailing ship makes for a serene and graceful weather vane. Moved by the wind, sailing-ship vanes seem almost as much in their element on their poles as they would be on the sea. Naturally, ship weather vanes are found almost exclusively along our country's coastline, particularly in the Northeast. There, the earliest ship vanes were made by amateur craftsmen and later by the vane manufacturers. Occasionally, one will be found further inland on the clubhouse of a yacht club situated on a large lake or river.

Most of the more ambitious ship weather vanes encountered today were made by the same breed of craftsmen who carved the ship models that grace many a New England mantelpiece. These were men who grew up near the sea and worked on sailing ships. They strove for authenticity in proportion, attitude, rigging, and the set of the sails.

The commercially produced ship weather vanes were not quite as successful from an artistic standpoint. The manufacturing considerations precluded the absolute fidelity to detail that could be worked into a completely handmade model. Also, the vane manufacturers had to be concerned about how well their models worked as weather vanes and perhaps made some compromises in design in favor of balance.

The earliest weather vanes with ship motifs were made of wood. Few have survived the long exposure to wind and weather. Many nineteenth-century vanes were cut from flat pieces of sheet metal and painted realistically. Full-rounded hollow copper ships appear to have been made only commercially either as stock items or on special orders. One of the few vanes of this type still being produced is a three-foot-long, relatively simple single-masted sloop that retails for $290 in natural copper and $380 when finished in twenty-three-carat gold leaf. Although it is in the catalogs of several suppliers, this sailboat is obviously being made from an old set of Washburne molds. A new ship model weather vane has recently been introduced that is eighteen inches long. It has a gold-leafed hull and white painted sails and sells for $85.

In the late nineteenth century the J. W. Fiske Company apparently endeavored to satisfy all possible markets by offering in their 1893 catalog in addition to a three-masted clipper ship of about an 1850 origin three ship models powered by steam: a ferry boat, a river steamer, and an ocean steamer. It is probable that these were especially commissioned for a shipping company's headquarters, and the drawings added to the catalog to attract a few more orders in hopes of amortizing the cost of the molds. Any of these steam-powered ship vanes would be extremely rare and valuable now. If they were executed to any degree toward the amount of detail shown in the drawings, they would be truly remarkable creations. Even the catalog renderings provide a fine historical record of a bygone era of water transportation.

The modern weather vanes with ship and boat motifs have gone back to the flat construction of the earliest ship vanes. Working in the simpler silhouette form, manufacturers can offer just about any type of vessel from a Viking dragon ship to a model of the tiny Sunfish sailboats. Boating enthusiasts have a wide selection of inexpensive vanes from which to choose. Most of these vanes are made from aluminum rather than copper, which was originally used for some of the older patterns.

Other subjects for weather vanes that are related to sailing and seamanship are also to be found. The Smithsonian Institution, in its Van Alstyne collection of American folk art, has a wood-carved horizontal figure of a sailor from a whaling ship blowing a horn.

The current catalog of Kenneth Lynch and Sons, Incorporated, shows two interesting nautical silhouette weather vanes. One is a peg-legged pirate peering through a telescope with the vane pointer shaped like two wave caps. The other is a sailor in a slicker and sou'wester hat also peering through a telescope. In the latter vane the front part of the telescope is also the pointer to the wind's direction.

This huge vane representing Henry
Hudson's ship "Half Moon" swings
high above the city of Albany, New York,
atop the Delaware and Hudson R. R.
building. Length twelve feet.

169

Weather vane of square-rigged ship.
Last half of nineteenth century.
Painted iron. Length: forty inches.
(*Smithsonian Institution*)

Ship vane on antique shop owned by
singer Lovelady Powell in Sag Harbor,
Long Island, New York. Vane is
handmade.

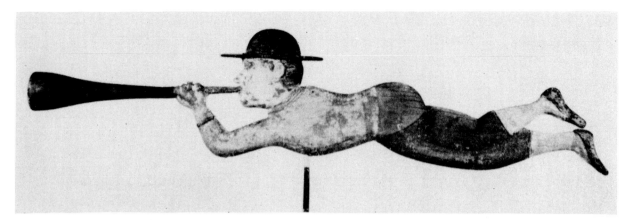

Whaler with horn vane made around
1875. Painted wood. Length:
forty-seven and a half inches.
(*Smithsonian Institution*)

Viking ship weather vane. Made in
copper by Garrett Thew Studios
around 1930.

COPPER
SILHOUETTE WEATHER VANES

Ship vane from Washburne 1920s catalog. Hull is sheet copper, one inch thick. Masts are round copper tubing. Length: thirty-six inches.

Wrought iron and copper gilt ship vane was designed and executed by W. Bainbridge Reynolds, Limited, in England in 1908 for Royal Naval College at Osborne, Isle of Wight.

Ocean steamer vane made by Fiske. Length: fifty-four inches.

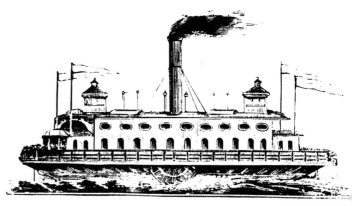

Ferryboat vane by Fiske. Length: thirty-six inches.

River steamer, made by Fiske in 1893. Length: forty-eight inches.

Silhouette vane of sailboat and seagulls
in East Hampton, Long Island

Ship vane on building at Southbury
Training School, Southbury, Connecticut.

Scull with waves and rower on vane on building adjoining Payne Whitney Gymnasium at Yale University. Made around 1920.

Copper vane made by Washburne in 1920s has been copied by makers to present day.

Pirate vane, aluminum vane painted or gold-leafed is modern and a Lynch design.

Silhouette vane, "Sou'wester," is vane that was made in wrought iron in 1930s but is currently being made in aluminum. Kenneth Lynch and Sons, Incorporated.

174

17

TRAINS AND FIRE ENGINES

The economic growth and expansion of the United States in the latter half of the nineteenth century was due in large measure to the rapid development of the American railway system, which was speeded by the gold rush of 1849. When the lines of the Union Pacific and the Central Pacific were finally joined on May 10, 1869, the country had accomplished what previously was thought to have been impossible. The entire country, from coast to coast, was joined by a rail network. The decade from 1880 to 1890 witnessed the most rapid railway expansion in the history of the United States, and until the end of World War I the railways had a virtual monopoly on transportation within the United States.

Concurrent with the building of the railways was, of course, the construction of stations in almost every town at which a train stopped. These buildings housed ticket agents and freight personnel and protected the traveler from inclement weather. The railway stations were designed in every architectural style that was popular in the late nineteenth century, and in many towns and cities the railway station was the outstanding architectural landmark for many years. In some cities and towns the local railroad station, often dilapidated and neglected, still stands as a memorial to the elegant period of railroad travel. A few of the stations still exhibit extravagant weather vanes in the shapes of the nineteenth-century locomotives and tenders that were masterpieces of metalcraft.

The three-dimensional train station weather vanes that were made to adorn the railway buildings are rare today and highly valued by weather-vane collectors and railway historians. They were very expensive when they were made and required intricate casting and assembly of the miniature parts, which were made to scale. The Fiske catalog for 1893 shows a locomotive and tender vane that could be purchased for what was at the time the great sum of $250. There are a few examples of locomotive and tender weather vanes that were probably made at an earlier date than the Fiske vane. One example is a vane that is cataloged in the *Index of American Design*. Probably made around 1870, it is owned by the Edison Institute of Technology and is nine feet long.

The Fiske locomotive and tender vane is advertised in the 1893 catalog as being available in a six-foot length. It is truly a scale model of the real locomotives that were used at the time and is meticulously detailed. All of the large, full-bodied copper vanes were made by hand, and something as intricate as a large locomotive made of copper, brass, and iron parts had to require the attention of a superb craftsman for many days. We can only be astounded by the detail of these great engine weather vanes and the work that went into them.

One of the earliest railway weather vanes that has been found is on display at the Shelburne Museum in Vermont. It is a two-dimensional silhouette vane and has a curious design of clouds and lightning above it. This vane came from Rhode Island and dates from around 1840, when railroad networks were being laid at a rapid rate along the eastern seaboard.

Silhouette weather vanes of locomotives were also made at lower cost for use on private homes and small railroad stations by Fiske in 1893. An interesting "Scroll and Locomotive" vane, advertised in the catalog, is a banneret with the silhouette of the locomotive cut into it. This vane was made in two sizes: four feet and six inches, and five feet. It might have been designed for railroad stations that did not warrant the expensive full-bodied vanes. This vane sold at the time for sixty and seventy dollars, depending upon the size.

By the time railroad locomotives became streamlined, the golden age of weather-vane manufacture was over, and new vanes do not seem to have been made in scale models of the streamlined trains of the 1930s. By this period, also, railroad stations were no longer being built. There are still a few weather-vane makers who are capable of reproducing the early locomotive weather vanes, but the cost today would be so prohibitive that it might discourage even the most affluent and dedicated railroad buff.

While the local railroad station served an important function in almost every town across the continent, the firehouse was even more vital to the existence of nineteenth-century communities. The bucket brigades of colonial times had developed into highly organized groups of fire fighters by the middle of the nineteenth century. During the late 1800s steam fire engines drawn by two or three horses provided most of the fire protection in towns across the United States. Gasoline-powered pumpers replaced the horse-drawn vehicles in the early 1900s, but it is the horse-drawn engines that appealed to the weather-vane designers, and they produced intricate scale models of them as vane decorations for firehouses. Other motifs associated with fire fighting were also used as weather-vane subjects in the late nineteenth century.

One superb example of a fire-fighting weather vane is still very much in use on the Barre, Vermont, firehouse. It is a full-round scale model of a horse-drawn hook and ladder, and it carries two drivers. This vane was probably made to order for the building on which it has stood for over eighty years. A similar vane is advertised in the 1893 Fiske Company catalog.

A giant horse-drawn steamer weather vane can be studied at closer range in the Shelburne Museum. It is eight feet long and was adapted from a real fire engine designed and made by Amoskeag Manufacturing Company in Manchester, New Hampshire. This realistic model of a steamer is made of brass, copper, zinc, and iron and is typical of the fire-fighting equipment used in this country in the late nineteenth century. The vane's immense proportions lead one to realize the great importance each town placed on its local firehouse, its men, and its equipment.

The Fiske catalog for 1893 also has examples of a variety of firehouse weather-vane motifs. One vane is a combination of a fireman's trumpet mounted on a shaft that is topped by a fireman's helmet.

Another Fiske vane is a ladder with two crossed hooks attached. Fiske's steam fire engine vane is advertised as "made to order in any size," and a seven-foot-long model sold in 1893 for $275. The hook and ladder previously mentioned is shown in the catalog but without horses or men. These were designed and made to order. Perhaps one of the most imaginative firehouse weather vanes made by Fiske is a figure of a fireman in three-quarter, full-bodied copper with one foot on the five-foot arrow vane and the other resting on the first rung of the ladder he is about to climb. He is holding a trumpet in his hand.

The elaborate weather vanes made to be used on both the railroad stations and the firehouses built in the nineteenth century are among the finest examples of American craftsmanship of the period. Few of them still exist today, and it is obvious that not many were made. However, any railroad weather vanes that have been made of recent date are in the genre of the early vanes. The Kenneth Lynch catalog of 1966 shows a drawing of a nineteenth-century horse-drawn engine that the Lynch Company was willing to make on special order. This engine is in full round and was at the time available in a thirty-two-inch length. Made of copper and bronze in nineteenth-century tradition, it is pulled by two horses that were painted white. The engine was painted in red and black. Nostalgia for the "good old days" has caused a few of these vanes to be ordered for recently built firehouses.

Locomotive with clouds and lightning.
Found in Rhode Island, vane dates
from 1840. Iron, sheet brass, and zinc.
Length: thirty-four inches; height:
thirty-six inches. (*Shelburne Museum*)

Amoskeag fire engine weather vane,
made between 1840 and 1880, is from
Manchester, New Hampshire. Length:
eight feet. Brass, copper, zinc, and
iron. (*Shelburne Museum*)

178

Silhouette locomotive weather vane in
Woodbury, Connecticut

Locomotive vane is on firehouse in
Northfield, Connecticut.

Locomotive on railroad station at Shelburne Museum is reproduction of vane in collection there.

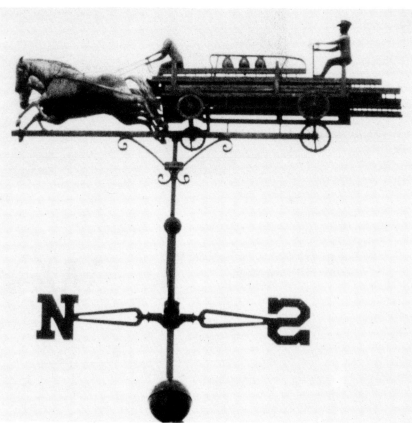

Copper vane is hook and ladder pulled by two horses. On firehouse in Barre, Vermont. Circa 1890.

Fire station in Tuckahoe, New York, shows vane of fireman's trumpet. Circa 1935.

Steam fire engine. Fiske would make any size to order.

Scroll and locomotive vane is six feet long. This vane was designed for the New York Elevated Railroad and put upon their station at South Ferry in New York City. It was a Fiske vane. End of nineteenth century.

Fireman's hat and trumpet, made in two sizes by Fiske. From 1893 catalog.

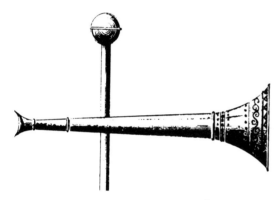

Fireman's trumpet vane. Length: two feet nine inches. Shown by Fiske in 1893 catalog.

Hook and ladder vane, shown by Fiske in 1893 catalog, came in six or seven-foot lengths.

Fireman vane, three-quarter, full-bodied copper. Height: thirty inches with five-foot arrow. Fiske.

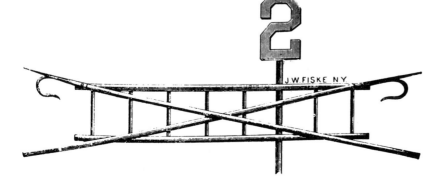

Steam fire engine silhouette weather
vane on firehouse in South Britain,
Connecticut.

Locomotive and tender vane. Length:
seventy-two inches. Fiske catalog,
1893.

18

TRADE SIGN
WEATHER VANES

A great many of the weather vanes that appear in previous chapters of this book were adaptations of trade signs. That is, they were visual announcements for products that were made within the buildings they adorned. A woolen mill used a large weather vane of a sheep; an abattoir might use a large version of the same hog or cow weather vane as the farmer who raised the animals used; a ship supply store might have ordered a full-rigged vessel to place atop its building; and an automobile dealer, having little knowledge in the early part of this century of how rapidly the contours of his product would change, might have ordered a full-bodied model of the product he sold.

The trade weather vane has its origins in the inn and tavern signs of England, and the use of the brightly painted signs continued in America for a long time. The small window panes used before the glassmakers had the ability to make large sheets of window glass precluded the customer from seeing what was going on inside a store, and the trade sign was an important advertisement for the merchant. Since the store owner couldn't count on his customers' ability to read, most trade signs were symbols or contained pictures of the goods made or sold on the premises. As store windows became larger, the small trade signs no longer swung freely over the heads of people walking past the stores, and larger signs with lettering were attached to the faces of buildings. The symbols of trade were relegated to the rooftops in the convenient forms of weather vanes.

Where there might not be an obvious symbol for a particular trade that would adapt easily to a vane, the craftsman used his imagination to design something that would announce what the activity inside a particular building might be. An interesting hand-crafted weather vane at Shelburne is a strong arm of a workman with a hammer in his fist. This vane was taken from the Delaware and Hudson Railroad car repair works in Carbondale, Pennsylvania, and it was made by Alec Wylie, a local blacksmith, in 1870. No other vanes attributable to this worker are known.

The late nineteenth-century weather-vane manufacturers, just as dependent upon their anvil as the village blacksmith, made weather vanes with anvil motifs. An anvil and arrow vane from the 1893 Fiske Company Catalog shows that this type of vane was still popular at that time. An anvil vane was also made by the Cushing Company.

The Fiske catalog has an illustration of a weather vane suitable for a shoe manufacturer. The vane, a two-foot-long high shoe in late nineteenth-century style, was mounted on a six-foot arrow and was obviously designed for use on a factory building, although the catalog states that Fiske would make the weather vane in "any size to order." One can surmise that some shoe merchants might have ordered this trade vane in a smaller size.

The tobacconist had his choice from the 1893 Fiske catalog of two suitable weather vanes that would advertise his profession. Both a tobacco leaf and a cigar were the two motifs available to him. Breweries could purchase from Fiske one of several suitable vanes for their buildings. A full-round figure of Gambrinus, the mythical Flemish king who is reputed to have been the inventor of beer, could be ordered in a three-foot nine-inch size or a five-foot size. Prices of these two vanes were $150 and $200. Other brewery vanes by Fiske had the motifs of a malt shovel and beer barrel, and the manufacturers could make vanes using one of these motifs or both together on the same shaft.

In the first half of this century the handsome trade weather vanes were replaced with garish neon and fluorescent lighted signs that advertised a product or service and could be seen for miles at night. Fortunately, this age too seems to be passing, and environmentalists will be happy to know that the trade sign weather vane from which a potential customer can from a distance associate exactly what is being offered for sale within a building is making a comeback.

At least one national grocery chain, the Great Atlantic and Pacific Tea Company, has developed a nationwide identity by topping its store buildings with arrow vanes that are decorated with their initials, A & P. This is all the customer has to see to identify immediately what store he is near. The Howard Johnson national food and motel chain has two trade sign weather vanes: one that is used on their motels, and another that identifies their restaurant buildings. When seen from a distance by a hungry and tired motorist, these silhouette vanes easily identify the services and products of a company that has long been part of the American scene. These weather vanes carry on a tradition of advertising that seems to be just as effective and certainly more attractive than flashing lighted signs.

At least one well-known fast food chain has begun to use a trade sign weather vane that has rapidly become familiar to American motorists. Within the past few years the white-suited figure of the "fried chicken king," Colonel Sanders, with his cane in hand, has been pointing the wind direction from the rooftops of his franchised drive-in stands. Other nationwide purveyors of goods and services have taken weather-vane motifs of more conventional shape. The Friendly ice cream and restaurant outlets use the rooster as the motif for their weather vanes, which top the three hundred restaurants that presently comprise their business. National gas companies have used other familiar motifs, such as the Mobil Oil Company's flying red horse, as part of the architecture for gas stations. Customers soon learn to identify any special weather vane as the symbol of a particular company.

If eagle and rooster vanes have become traditional symbols of America's past, there is at least one modern weather vane that is, perhaps, the ultimate American trade sign vane. This vane is a silhouette of the dollar sign atop a farm credit office in a shopping center in Wethersfield, Connecticut. On seeing it, one has little doubt of the product that is being "sold" within.

Anvil weather vane. Iron and zinc, painted yellow ochre. Length: twenty-four inches. Late nineteenth century. (*Shelburne Museum*)

Blacksmith's sign and weather vane. Height: forty-seven inches. Delaware and Hudson Railroad, Carbondale, Pennsylvania. Made by Alec Wylię in 1870. (*Shelburne Museum*)

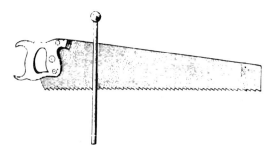

Saw, carpenter's trade sign vane, made by Fiske in 1893. Vane was made in any size to order.

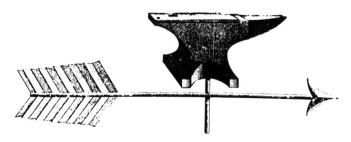

Anvil and arrow vane made by Fiske in 1893. Length: six feet.

Shoe and arrow vane, six feet long, by Fiske. From 1893 catalog.

Cigar, tobacconist's trade sign vane. Length: thirty-six inches. From 1893 Fiske catalog.

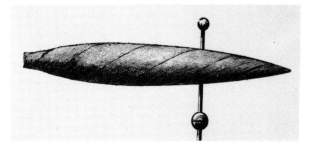

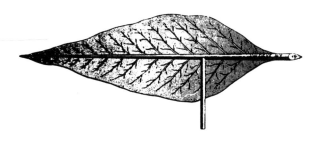

Tobacco leaf. Length: four feet. Made by Fiske in late nineteenth century.

Bicyclist and arrow vane advertised messenger service in late nineteenth century. From 1893 Fiske catalog.

Gambrinus vane was made by Fiske in 1893 in two sizes: three feet nine inches and five feet. Gambrinus was legendary monarch who was supposed to have invented beer.

Welch Farms trade sign weather vane.

One of variety of styles used by
A & P. All are arrows or pennants.

Weather vane trade sign, fiber glass,
advertising fried chicken stands.

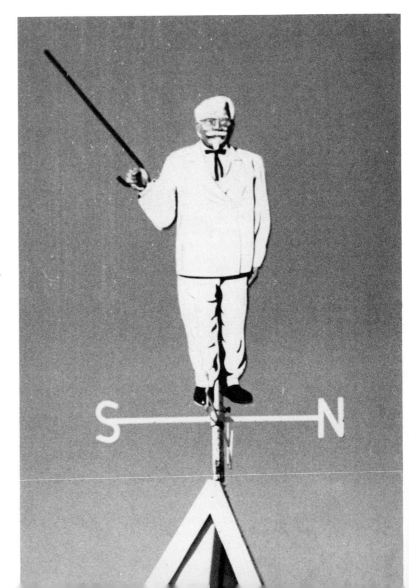

190

Howard Johnson's easily recognized
trade sign weather vane used on
restaurants

Weather vane used on Howard Johnson
motels

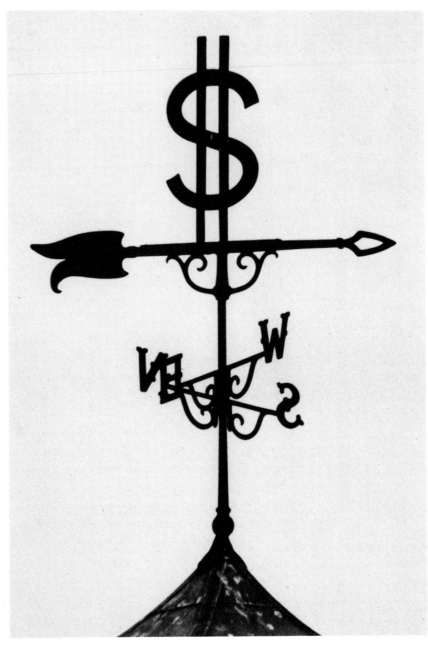

Modern trade sign vane on Farm Credit
Building in Wethersfield, Connecticut

192

19

WIND TOYS

Man's ability to harness the wind and make it work for him to pump water, grind wheat, saw wood, and perform other tasks probably had its western origins in the twelfth century when windmills were first used in Europe. It is thought that the device was learned from the Arabs and the idea brought back by the Crusaders. The wind, of course, was used to move vessels on the water from ancient times. The use of the wind to move devices made simply for amusement is even more ancient, however. The Chinese have for many centuries hung devices outside their doorways that would make pleasant sounds when the breezes blew.

Toys that have movement have long been a source of amusement for adults as well as children. One of the most ancient of wind toys, the pinwheel on a stick, is still a delight to small children. It is probable that the earliest wind toys made in this country were simple pinwheel devices that could be attached to buildings or trees. Many probably served the additional purpose of acting as scarecrows to frighten birds from the garden.

By the middle of the eighteenth century small figures were carved with propellers for arms that would twirl frantically when the wind caught them. It is probable that this form of wind toy, which only recently has been referred to as a whirligig, was brought to this country by European wood-carvers. Few of these earliest forms of folk art have survived, but the custom of carving figures or other moving toys that could somehow be propelled by wind power prevailed throughout the nineteenth century and into this century.

Some of the methods of incorporating propellers that would revolve into the figure of a whirligig are ingenious. On most single-figure whirligigs the arms or some hand-held instruments are the wind devices. On other more elaborate toys the vanes are simply to one side and are attached to a mechanism that moves the figure.

Nineteenth-century whirligigs were all creations of the home craftsman who required little else in the way of tools and material than a stick or two of wood and his pocket knife. Although the single human figure was most often used, more ambitious artists devised complicated creations that still amuse their viewers today.

Since the whirligigs were made simply for pleasure and had no function except to amuse passersby or to decorate the garden, few were made that had any permanence, and not too many from the early period survive today. Those that we do find represent the true folk art of the immigrant wood-carver and the work of the Yankee whittler to whom idle hands were sinful. The whirligig figures of the nineteenth and early twentieth centuries that are one-of-a-kind folk sculptures are full-figured carvings that were originally brightly painted or decorated in some way.

One mid-nineteenth-century whirligig on display at the Shelburne Museum is an Indian figure carved of wood with tinfoil embellishments that represent his clothing and headdress. The arms extend into propellers that caught the wind and twirled. This figure was probably adapted from the cigar store Indians that were prevalent tobacconists' trade signs during the period in which it was made.

Another Shelburne figural whirligig dating from 1870 is a swordsman with a wide grin on his carved wooden face. He is holding a sword in each of his hands which are the propellers, and, like Don Quixote, this figure was destined to strike out forever at the wind without destroying the enemy.

A washerwoman whirligig illustrated in this chapter is also a Shelburne acquisition, and it is a marvel of mechanical folk art. Found in Ohio, this carved figure with apron and bonnet is twelve inches high. When the windmill device at the side of the toy was caught by the wind, it turned a series of gears that caused the washerwoman perpetually to scrub over her washboard. The toy is made mainly of wood and zinc and is brightly painted. As long as the winds blew, the poor woman was destined to scrub and scrub, and the painted expression on her face would lead one to believe that she was fully aware of her fate.

A late nineteenth-century whirligig made of wood and tin is also an ingenious device that would keep the predominant figure at work as long as the wind would propel him. This toy represents a cyclist mounted on a metal circle. As long as the side propeller turned, the cyclist was destined to travel forever the same circular route.

Other diabolical whittlers and home craftsmen found means of keeping whirligig figures constantly on the move. Dancing figures could never stop as long as there was the slightest breeze. Other mechanical whirligigs kept a figure hard at work chopping or sawing the same piece of wood, and miniature carved figures of policemen never stopped waving their long arms.

Although many of them are not very old, the handmade whirligigs have become recognized as important examples of American folk art and are being preserved and displayed as such in many museums. Since these charming wind toys were not made to last through centuries of wind and weather, it is necessary that they be brought indoors where their preservation will be assured. Whittling and carving in wood is fast becoming a lost art, and the present surge of interest in American handcrafted artifacts has led to the preservation of at least some of these charming folk sculptures.

Even the more complicated mechanical whirligigs made in this century are well worth preserving, since they display imaginative design as well as a sense of humor. The elaborate Ferris wheel illustrated in this chapter is an example of a whirligig–weather-vane combination that was probably made in the first quarter of this century. It must have taken hours of work and patience on the part of its creator. It is an amusing simplification of the object it portrays. The figures are represented only through the use of carved and painted heads, but the overall effect is realistic enough to represent the subject adequately.

It does not appear that whirligigs were ever made commercially until recently, when plastic wind toys came on the market. These lack the charm of the handmade wooden whirligigs. A search in the catalogs of the nineteenth- and early twentieth-century weather-vane makers has only turned up one example of anything that might approximate a whirligig–weather-vane combination. This is a Washburne engraving of a miniature windmill atop a silhouette vane of a farmer and his dog. At a cost of $120 in the 1920s, this whirligig–vane with the windmill in full-round gilded or bronzed copper could hardly be considered a "wind toy," but it is in the same genre.

Magazines for home craftsmen published in the twenties and thirties gave patterns for making simple whirligig figures from planks of wood. These were drawn from patterns onto the boards and cut out with a jigsaw and then painted and assembled according to directions. These later whirligigs did not require any special skills on the part of the makers. However, even these figures are fast disappearing from the American landscape. Indians with paddle-arms that perpetually rowed a canoe and little Dutch-style windmills were the patterns most often used. During the Depression these plank-type whirligigs could be found for sale along many roads in America, since they were inexpensive to make and required little or no talent on the part of the maker.

The story of whirligigs or wind toys seems to have come full circle. The good handcrafted examples have found their way to private collections and museums that display American folk art. The modern wind toys we find in use today are imported replicas of the earliest devices made to capture the wind just for enjoyment. The Oriental wind toys that are hung outside to make pleasant tinkling sounds when the wind blows them decorate many American doorways.

The nonutilitarian whirligigs are no longer a part of the American scene, but the weather vane, itself an anachronism in this age of scientific weather forecasting, has become so much a part of our architecture that it will continue to be made as long as there are dedicated craftsmen who are willing to take the time and effort necessary to produce them. Americans will, it seems, always want to know which way the wind is blowing.

Naval figure whirligig. Made around 1820. Carved wood. Originally from Falmouth, Massachusetts. Height: thirty-seven inches. (*Shelburne Museum*)

196

Washerwoman whirligig. Height: twelve inches. Wood and zinc, painted. From Ohio. Made around 1850. (*Shelburne Museum*)

Whirligig, Negro figure. Found in St. Albans, Vermont. Height: eighteen inches. Nineteenth century. (*Shelburne Museum*)

Cyclist whirligig. Wood and tin. Height: sixteen and a half inches. Late nineteenth century. (*Shelburne Museum*)

Indian whirligig. Wood and tinfoil. Height: seventeen and three-eighths inches. From New York State. Made around 1850. (*Shelburne Museum*)

Swordsman whirligig. Painted wood. Made about 1870. Height: eighteen inches. (*Shelburne Museum*)

Goose-in-flight whirligig. Wood carving. Length: thirty-seven inches. Nineteenth century. (*Shelburne Museum*)

Whirligig, World War I doughboy with gun. Painted wood. (*Shelburne Museum*)

Weather vane and windmill combination.
Rod with silhouette of dog and fence.
Length: forty-two inches. Washburne
catalog of 1920.

Ferris wheel whirligig. Hand-carved
and hand-painted. Front propeller is
missing. (*Ross Levett*)

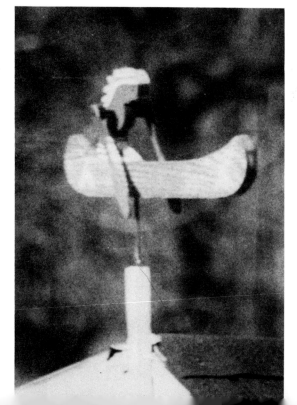

Indian in canoe made
around 1930. Painted wood.

BIBLIOGRAPHY

Allen, E. B. "Old American Weathervanes." *International Studio* 80 (1925): 450–453.
"The Useful and Agreeable." *Time*, September 27, 1954, p. 80.
"Vanes." *New Yorker*, September 12, 1964, 39–40.
Buckert, Ilse, and Nesbitt, Alexander. *Weathervanes and Weathercreatures*. Newport, Rhode Island: Third and Elm Press, 1970.
Christensen, Erwin O. *The Index of American Design*. New York: Macmillan National Gallery of Art; Washington, D.C., Smithsonian Institution: 1950.
Eaton, Allen H. *Handicrafts of New England*. New York: Bonanza Books, 1959.
Fiske, J. W. *Illustrated Catalogue and Price List of Copper Weathervanes and Finials*. New York, 1893.
Fitzgerald, Ken. *Weathervanes and Whirligigs*. New York: Clarkson N. Potter, 1967.
Hornung, Clarence P. *Treasury of American Design*. New York: Abrams, 1972.
Hawthorne, Nathaniel. "Drowne's Wooden Image." In *Mosses from an Old Manse*. Boston: Houghton Mifflin, 1882.
Jenkins, Dorothy H. "Weathervanes." In *Woman's Day*, July 1968, pp. 85–86.
Kaye, Myrna. "Hark: The Herald Angel." *Yankee*, December 1966, pp. 42–44.
Klamkin, Charles. *Barns: Their History, Preservation and Restoration*. New York: Hawthorn, 1972.
Lipman, Jean. *American Folk Art in Wood, Metal and Stone*. New York: Pantheon, 1948.
Lynch, Kenneth, and Sons, Inc. *Garden Ornaments, General Wholesale Catalog for the Trade*. Number 2066. Wilton, Connecticut, 1966.
———. *Weather Vanes, Catalog Number 20*. 215 East 42nd St., New York, New York. N.D. (about 1938).
Parke-Bernet Galleries. *Catalog of the American Heritage Society Auction of Americana*. New York, November 12–13, 1971.
Thomas, John and Betty. "Vanishing Vanes." *Sunday Times-Union*: Albany, New York. August, 31, 1969. B–7.
Vallance, Aymer. "British Stained Glass, Pottery, and Metalwork." *The Studio Yearbook of Decorative Art*. London. 1908. 26, B228.
Washburne, E. G. and Company, *Catalogue of Copper Silhouette Vanes*. 207 Fulton Street, New York. N.D. (about 1930).
———. *Illustrated Catalogue and Price List of Copper Weathervanes*. 207 Fulton Street, New York. N.D. (about 1920).
Wellman, Rita. "American Weathervanes." *House Beautiful*. January 1939, pp. 50–54, 69.
Welsh, Peter C. *American Folk Art, The Art and Spirit of a People, From the Eleanor and Mabel Van Alstyne Collection*. Washington, D.C.: Smithsonian Institution, 1965.